Twayne's United States Authors Series

Sylvia E. Bowman, *Editor*
INDIANA UNIVERSITY

Louis Simpson

LOUIS SIMPSON

By RONALD MORAN

University of North Carolina
at Chapel Hill

Twayne Publishers, Inc.   ::   New York

To

my Mother and to the memory of my Father

Preface

More, perhaps, than any other poet of his generation, Louis Simpson has come to terms directly and fully with defining what America has meant and currently means. In addition, Simpson has emerged as a major literary interpreter of World War II. A number of his early lyrics are exemplary of superior achievement within the exacting boundaries of formal tradition. However, he abandoned close adherence to the conventions in favor of a looser, more colloquially based and imaginative style, thus marking him as a pioneer in a distinctly new and significant movement in American poetry.

This is the first book-length study about Simpson; and though its main intent is to stress Simpson's works, the first chapter traces events in his life that have exerted major influences on his writings. Chapters 2 through 7 are devoted to examining the poems included in his six volumes of poetry. Each of these chapters is subdivided primarily into the subject areas of inquiry in which Simpson has worked most consistently. Chapter 8 analyzes his only published novel; the study concludes with an appraisal of his literary contributions.

I am grateful to the Office of Research Administration of the University of North Carolina at Chapel Hill for a grant that enabled me to undertake research during the summer of 1967. I should also like to express my gratitude to Louis Simpson for his generosity in allowing me access to information otherwise unavailable.

RONALD MORAN

The University of North Carolina
at Chapel Hill

Acknowledgments

Louis Simpson's poems quoted herein are copyright © 1949, 1956, 1957, 1958, 1959, 1960, 1961, 1962, and 1963 by Louis Simpson, from his books *A Dream of Governors* and *At the End of the Open Road;* reprinted by permission of Wesleyan University Press. The following poems first appeared in *The New Yorker:* "The Green Shepherd," "The Sea and the Forest" (as "Sailors"), "The Silent Lover," "The Redwoods," and "My Father in the Night Commanding No."

Excerpts from *The Arrivistes* by Louis Simpson are reprinted by his permission.

Excerpts from poems by Louis Simpson are reprinted with the permission of Charles Scribner's Sons from *Good News of Death and Other Poems* by Louis Simpson. (Copyright 1955 Louis Simpson) POETS OF TODAY II.

Excerpts from "Tonight the Famous Psychiatrist," "The Tailor's Wedding," "Things," "Stumpfoot on 42nd Street" and "In the Time of Villa" © 1965 by Louis Simpson, from *Selected Poems* by Louis Simpson; reprinted by permission of Harcourt Brace Jovanovich, Inc.

"Outward," © 1965 by Louis Simpson, from *Selected Poems* by Louis Simpson; reprinted by permission of Harcourt Brace Jovanovich, Inc.

"The Wall Test" and "American Dreams" are reprinted from Louis Simpson's *Adventures of the Letter I* by permission of Oxford University Press.

Acknowledgments

These poems are reprinted by permission. Acknowledgment is made to the publishers in which these poems first appeared.

Contents

Chronology

1923 Louis Aston Marantz Simpson born in Kingston, Jamaica,
British West Indies, March 27, son of Aston and Rosalind
Marantz Simpson.

1940 Arrived in New York City; entered Columbia University.

1942– Served in the United States Army with 101st Airborne Di-
1945 vision. Received Bronze Star with an oak-leaf cluster and
two Purple Hearts.

1948 Bachelor of Science, School of General Studies, Columbia
University.

1948– In Paris.
1949

1949 *The Arrivistes: Poems 1940–1949.* Married Jeanne C. Rogers.

1950 Master of Arts in English, Columbia University. Began
working for Bobbs-Merrill Publishing Company in New
York City.

1954 Divorced.

1955 *Good News of Death and Other Poems.* Began teaching on
a full-time basis in Department of English, Columbia College. Married Dorothy M. Roochvarg.

1957– Awarded *Prix de Rome* for poetry. Appointed *Hudson Re-
1958 view* Fellow in Poetry. In Rome.

1959 *A Dream of Governors.* Doctor of Philosophy in Comparative Literature, Columbia University. Began teaching in
Department of English, University of California, Berkeley.

1960 Received Distinguished Service Award, School of General
Studies, Columbia University.

1962 *Riverside Drive. James Hogg, A Critical Study.*

1963 *At the End of the Open Road* (Pulitzer Prize for Poetry).
Appointed Guggenheim Fellow. In Great Britain and Italy.

1965 *Selected Poems.* Awarded Medal for Excellence, Columbia
University.

1967   *An Introduction to Poetry.* Began teaching in Department
       of English, State University of New York at Stony Brook.
1970– Appointed Guggenheim Fellow. In London.
1971
1971   *Adventures of the Letter I.*

CHAPTER *1*

The American from Jamaica

I *Jamaica*

IN a 1964 essay about four distinguished poets who once attended Columbia University, Louis Aston Marantz Simpson is cited as saying: "Poems spring from the inner life of a poet. Therefore, nearly everything depends on the kind of man he is." [1] In the same year, shortly after he was awarded the Pulitzer Prize for Poetry for his fourth collection of poems, *At the End of the Open Road*, Simpson tells the interviewer for *dust* magazine that a "writer ought to have a lot of experiences, and particularly emotional experiences." To Simpson, the writer "has to feel, he has to learn how to feel, and you can't learn these things without a few disasters. You have to see the bottom side of life. We have had some writers who never saw the bottom side of life, of course, but most good writers have seen a range of human behavior. But you can't just go and look at it as an observer; you have to live it. You have to be subjected to it." [2] If emotional experiences are germane in providing the basic ingredients for a significant writer, then Simpson's early years certainly qualify him. These years were by no means pleasant ones for the poet; but, as he suggests in the *dust* interview, a life without experiencing a "wide range of human behavior" is not conducive to forming a good writer.

Louis Simpson was born in Kingston, Jamaica, British West Indies, on March 27, 1923. His father was Aston Simpson, a Kingston lawyer of Scotch ancestry whom the poet has often described as a practical man. Simpson's mother was Rosalind Marantz whose family were Polish Jews from Lutsk who emigrated to the United States before World War I. When Rosalind Marantz was twelve years old, she was entrusted to bring the remaining children from Poland to New York where her mother had already gone with an older child. [3] In New York Rosalind "worked in the sweat shops of the garment district, and conceived such a loathing for the work, and immigrants too, that it determined the rest of her life." She dreamed, the poet recalls, of being a prima donna; and the opportunity to fulfill her dream presented itself in the role as one of Annette Kellerman's bathing beauties. While the troupe was on location in Jamaica filming a movie, she met attorney Aston Simpson, who followed her to New York, courted her, and brought her back to Kingston as his bride.

The Simpsons bought a home near Cross Roads in the suburbs of Kingston and "lived as well-to-do colonials," which Simpson explains, "required an establishment of four to five servants—a cook, housemaid, Nannie, garden-boy, and chauffeur." Despite the lawn parties, piano lessons for the children (Simpson has an older brother, Herbert), and the like, the poet claims that the family did not blend into colonial life: "As I grew up I had a sense of being outside normal society—that 'alienation' which is so typical of modern artists that it has become a joke." Simpson continues that this alienation resulted in part from the family's being neither of the peasant nor the governing class. With Rosalind's unusual background, his mother was not well suited to Jamaican middle-class life: "In the torpid society of Kingston, with its lawn-tennis parties, she remained an exotic."

His mother's penchant for fairy tales and for telling the children stories at night after they had been put to bed by the "nannie" remains in the poet's memory. She told "stories of her childhood in Poland, of snow and wolves, and the rats that swarmed during a famine; or else she read us fairytales." And Rosalind Marantz was passionately devoted to opera: "when I was old enough to wind the gramophone I would listen to opera 'gems' and turn the pages of the 'Victor Book of the Opera' with photographs of the opera houses of Milan, Paris and San Francisco." Simpson claims that his mother's stories gave his mind a "turn for fantasy I have never been able to overcome." One of his finest poems, "My Father in the Night Commanding No," is drawn primarily from recollections of his mother and her stories and of his father, who was "full of silent ratiocination." This curious combination—a mother with a mind for fairy tales and a father with a passion for facts—has led Simpson to remark that "these may have been a beginning of poetry. . . ."

An incident happened when Simpson was four or five that, he

supposes, could account for his interest in poetry. One night his father set up a telescope on a tripod and held the children up by turns to look through it, at which time the boy became "moonstruck and devoted to poetry, though my father . . . would have been surprised to know it." [4] Simpson remembers the experience this way: "In the moon, rising round and silver-white about the Blue Mountains, I thought I saw, or was persuaded to see, the bearded king, George V, like the profile on his shilling. While lizards hopped from the vine onto the railing of the verandah, casting dragon shadows on the walls, and frogs croaked in the garden, the moon returned through a million stars toward Scotland and Poland, whose spirits had been bound, by an enchantment of marriage, in these tropics." But the enchantment did not last, and when Simpson was six or seven, his parents were divorced. His mother returned to New York; the poet and his brother remained in Kingston with their father.

From the age of nine to seventeen, Simpson attended Munro College, a preparatory school in the mountains of St. Elizabeth where his brother Herbert also went. The boys spent their vacations with their father, who, after he remarried, moved to a new house near Bournemouth on the harbor. Simpson has rarely said anything about his stepmother, who gave to Aston Simpson two additional children: a girl, Molly, and a boy, John. The poet writes of these years at the school in the mountains with ambivalent feelings.

Munro College was run strictly. Some of his teachers, Simpson recalls, were "sadists, but none of them were ignorant." He says that "Beating and bullying were ordinary" and that the younger boys learned early to take their lumps, whether physical or emotional, without complaining; for there was no one to whom the students could turn for sympathy, certainly not to the teachers: "What the system inculcated was a lively instinct of self-preservation. . . . We learned to fight, and never to cry, and we learned to laugh with the master and jeer at the victim—the boy who couldn't add and subtract, or stuttered, or blushed cherry-red. We were intolerant of cowardice and timidity, or any eccentricity of body or mind." Yet the school did have its advantages, both for the students in general and for Simpson in particular. No discrimination based on class, color, or money was permitted. And any boy could gain the respect of his masters and peers alike if he excelled in sports or, in the higher forms, if he distinguished himself as a student. The poet did very well on both counts.

A great advantage to Simpson was the emphasis the school placed on reading and writing. He remembers being taught literature by a "Scotsman whose rendition of 'Macbeth' was hair-raising"; of being taught Racine and Molière by a Frenchman; but, above all, of being forced "to write on every subject." Simpson, who learned to be an avid reader, read what the library at Munro College offered; and he used his pocket money to send to England for more books: "It took two months, at least, for a book to arrive. When it came I would read it in a corner or take it out on the commons, and lie under a tree, with clouds streaming over to the plains and sea below." His interest in reading, which was in no way forced on him, led to his desire to write: "There were things I had dreamed of that were not in the books. So I began writing. But I did not intend to be a poet. I wanted to tell stories. I wanted to use words that would bring other people under a spell and win their admiration. Writing came as naturally as playing games."

Simpson was about fourteen or so when he began his headlong plunge into writing, which included not only stories but also poems. In fact, he published his first piece—a prize-winning essay about the coronation of George VI which was printed by the *Daily Gleaner*, a Kingston newspaper—during the first year of his writing. The next year he wrote a story which won a prize and was subsequently printed in the same paper. Aside from such encouragement, his creative writing was stimulated by the internal political strife in Jamaica between the natives and the colonial government. His sympathies lay with the insurgents, perhaps, he explains, because "history" finally was happening on the island. He also speculates on another, deeper reason: "The colonial habit of leaving children to the care of Nannies and garden boys led, by a kind of justice, to their feeling with the servants. If the battle of Waterloo was won on the playing fields of Eton, the Empire was lost in the nursery." The revolution was occurring when the poet was in his teens; and, when he was about sixteen, Simpson fell in with a group of prep-school boys "who had discovered the heady, prep-school socialism of the Oxford poets." As a result, he began to write poems and stories for *Public Opinion*, a liberal newspaper. Though Simpson says his literary tastes at the time lay with Joseph Conrad and Thomas Hardy rather than with Oxford poets (e.g., W. H. Auden, Louis MacNeice, and Stephen Spender), he reasons that he was welcomed by the liberal student writers since "writers were so rare" in Jamaica.

Simpson's participation in the revolution made him increasingly aware of the inequities of prejudice: "A group of us, we were seventeen to twenty or so, were writing for the newspaper [*Public Opinion*]. There was shooting in the streets and I was riding my bicycle distributing the newspaper in all this. I saw the Negro-white thing there, and I never had any problem taking sides. I'm for integration as fast as possible. . . . I think that the reason I'm for it, apart from my particular love of the Negro, is for my own future, the future of everyone. I feel we should do this as fast as possible." [5]

Two additional incidents in his childhood remain firmly embedded in the poet's mind. His father had crudely put together a motor boat in which the family cruised from Kingston to Port Royal and back again. One Christmas morning, as the Simpsons were about to leave the harbor, they noticed that an excursion launch with about forty natives on it had disappeared. When the father circled to the spot, all that remained was a hat or two floating on the water. The excursion launch had capsized, and everyone had drowned. This mass drowning suggests to Simpson a Naturalistic view of the universe which is not unlike that expressed by Stephen Crane in his short story, "The Open Boat." As Simpson sees the inherent alienation between man and the universe he inhabits, "The sadness of the provinces [Jamaica] is the thought of life vanishing without a mark. The pellucid sky neither sees nor cares. In the indifference of nature, you are terribly alone. Men are alone in cities too, but they are distracted by the crowd; and all those solitudes, pressing against one another, form the illusion of a common experience, a human condition, which absorbs and—who knows—may even depend on, the loneliness of the individual."

The other influential incident, which, like the drowning of the natives, has been incorporated into Simpson's novel, *Riverside Drive*, involves the poet's first love—a girl he met when he was about twelve years old. She moved, the poet remembers, in and out of his dreams for years, and he credits her with providing the driving force which led him to excel at Munro College: "Stimulated by the vision, I worked and played in a euphoria which, as no neo-platonist would be surprised to hear, led to my outstripping my companions, taking first place in examinations, getting letters for boxing, gymnastics and target shooting. . . . Once she went with me, and her puling brother, to a movie at the Carib Theater, a big, new palace in the American style. The movie was *The Firefly,* and to this day the 'Donkey Serenade' revives in me the leaping or fainting pulse of those hours."

At Munro College, Simpson passed the Cambridge Higher Schools Certificate; but he remained at the school in order to take the examinations again for a possible scholarship to Oxford. Then Aston Simpson died, and a few days later the poet and his brother learned that they had been virtually disinherited and that the vast majority of their father's estate had been willed to the second wife. In the summer of 1940, Simpson left for New York to visit his mother; and he has never returned to the island: "And I could never go back, for I might find myself, as in a dream, compelled to remain there, forever separated from the continent. Yet the mountains and sea and clouds are imprinted on my mind. . . . And I am still troubled by the islander's illusion, that somewhere else, in the supreme capital city, life is always interesting and meaningful; in that real world, men are brave and loyal and witty, and women are beautiful."

II *America*

Arriving in America was the most significant event in Louis Simpson's literary life. Although it was not until the 1950's that he began to write poems that set out to embody America—its history, its landscapes, its spirit—and to define contemporary American life to the extent that he has become a major interpreter of America, Simpson was immediately aware in 1940 of the dynamic possibilities intrinsic in the country. Asked by the *dust* interviewer if becoming an American had "some special meaning" for his work as a poet, Simpson replies:

> I think I had to become an American. As I told you, I worked for *Public Opinion,* which was anti-English and trying to promote Jamaican independence. We broke with the English system, you see, and at that time I broke with it in my own mind, as a writer.

Then, for personal reasons I couldn't stay in Jamaica. So I came to the States. That was the direction I had to go in, and once I came here I became very interested in the country because so much seemed possible. America is still a dynamic, changing society, only we don't know where we're going. I like America. It's still a place of opportunities, which people don't seem to realize.

Simpson continues that, when he first arrived in America, "every street was really very exciting, all the little things that Americans take for granted." And, when asked by the *dust* interviewer if America had advanced the writing of his poetry, Simpson's enthusiastic reply testifies to the emotional vitality that underscores his poems, particularly those from the late 1950's on that place him as one of America's foremost poets:

Oh, yes. It may be that the things I say about America are foolish to one who was born here, but I'm fascinated with America. There are all sorts of things that haven't been written about. That's what is so exciting to me. I would like to write a poem that would make you say, "Boy, that's the first time anyone ever described a gas station!" I was writing it, but it didn't work out; another poem worked out instead. I was talking about a filling station at night when a whole town is closed down, and I wrote: "The lights of the filling station were quivering with emotion." Now, that's what they were doing. All the other lights are out as you arrive in this strange town, and you see the white lights, the gas pump lights, quivering with emotion.[6]

In September, 1940, after having abandoned the British system and the thought of attending Oxford University on a scholarship, Simpson enrolled at Columbia University. He first joined the staffs of the *Columbian* and *Jester;* then, in 1941, he joined the staff of the *Review* and became its editor the following year: "Those days, or rather nights, I used to stay up writing till dawn broke over Amsterdam Avenue." He was not certain while at Columbia about what he was going to do with his education or, in fact, what he was even doing at the university. Simpson was only certain that he wanted to read and to write incessantly. Simpson's teachers at Columbia included Lionel Trilling, Raymond Weaver, and Mark Van Doren, the one who made the deepest impression on Simpson and of whom he says: "He knew what poetry was about. He made us feel it and see it."[7] Van Doren's importance to Simpson is recorded in the student's dedication of his first book, *The Arrivistes,* to his teacher.

III *War*

On a January morning in 1943 and during the middle of his junior year at Columbia, Louis Simpson was inducted into the United States Army. After indoctrination at Fort Dix in New Jersey, he was sent to Texas, assigned to a tank regiment, and listed as a loader and radioman.[8] His prewar experiences in the army have led Simpson to state that the "aim of military training is not just to prepare men for battle, but to make them long for it." The obsessive rituals of inspection and drill, the tedious routines, the mismatched training programs—these Simpson cites as some of the methods by which the military makes one "long" for battle.

At Fort Hood in Texas, Simpson was re-educated: "The iron of which those tanks were made entered our souls. Hood was our university. There we got our real education, which set us off from the men who came before and the men who came after. Sometimes in speaking to older men I have sensed there is a veil between us; and to a man of twenty-five, there are things I cannot explain." Then, after extensive training in iron, Simpson was taken out of the tank corps and put into specialized engineering training—a change in training which he calls "a fraction of the sum of waste, the incalculable extravagance of war."

After a brief stay at Louisiana State University in Baton Rouge for an interlude in engineering, the poet was sent to an infantry division at Fort Leonard Wood in Missouri; the particular outfit to which he was assigned within the division was, he asserts, a "kind of factory for turning out infantry replacements who would go overseas." Shortly after he arrived in Missouri, Simpson was shipped overseas to join the 101st Airborne Division, and he served with it in combat in France, Holland, Belgium, and Germany. The early chapters of his novel, *Riverside Drive,* provide a vivid, meaningful account of his combat experiences; moreover, Simpson has also written the best war poems that have derived from World War II experiences. Since both the novel and the poems are discussed in subsequent chapters, this chapter emphasizes only what Simpson has written in factual prose about his experiences.

"Action," the poet maintains, "was better" than training. In training, he and others always anticipated combat and, in so doing, were "oppressed by many anxieties." In combat, however, he "confronted the worst and could hope for an end of things." For his "action," Simpson received the Bronze Star with an oak-leaf cluster, two Purple Hearts, and a Presidential Unit Citation. He was involved in some of the bitterest fighting of the European campaign. His essay "The Making of a Soldier USA" concludes impressionistically with Simpson's drawing from personal experience to dramatize what he means by the statement that the military, through prewar training, makes men anxious to be involved in combat. Despite being wounded in a graveyard in Verghel, Holland, he was told to function as a runner to take messages back and forth from headquarters to the front line: "I get to my feet and run crouching between the graves. I'm aware of explosions all around and a humming of jagged iron. But I have a strange feeling of joy. I've been tagged already—I'm safe. But more than this, I'm exhilarated at the prospect of doing something."

"The Way It Was In the Bulge," a 1964 essay in the *New York Times Magazine,* relates Simpson's service with the 101st Airborne Division in the defense of Bastogne. His account tells nothing of glory or heroism; rather, it stresses frozen feet; the following of orders that seemed senseless; the digging of foxholes, then the leaving to dig foxholes in another field or on the side of another hill as soon as the first were dug; the sounds of guns, tank tracks, and planes: "That was the defense of Bastogne—standing in a hole in the snow, or lying down in the snow, for hours and days." During the battle in the Ardennes—Hitler's last offensive maneuver—Simpson once again acted as a runner, from which he gained the source material for his longest poem, "The Runner," a blank-verse narrative which, the poet says, is fiction: "the episodes and characters are imaginary." However, he does state in a prefatory note to the poem that the fiction is based upon the defense of Bastogne by the 101st Airborne Division. As a runner himself, Simpson feels that "however humbly" he had "something to do with the intelligence that directed battles, if intelligence there was." [9]

IV *After the War*

Louis Simpson concludes "The Heroes," an ironic poem on returning war heroes, with this stanza:

> A fine dust has settled on all that scrap metal.
> The heroes were packaged and sent home in parts
> To pluck at a poppy and sew on a petal
> And count the long night by the stroke of their hearts.

Shortly after being honorably discharged from the army in time
to return to his studies at Columbia for the 1946 spring term,
Simpson suffered a "complete delayed combat fatigue" and spent
six months in a mental institution, which he calls a "concentration
camp." [10] Although Duncan Bell, the main character of *Riverside
Drive*, is also committed to a mental hospital following his return
from the war, Simpson says that he refers only "slightly" in the
novel to his own commitment. Since Simpson also suffered from
amnesia, he is unable to recall completely what he experienced in
the hospital, but he remembers enough, he tells the *dust* interviewer, to say he saw "things there that were the worst you can
imagine." Once he saw a young Negro boy, about nineteen years
old, who was beaten to death by two guards who later threatened
to see that the poet would remain in the institution for life if he
told the authorities what he had witnessed. So, naturally, he did
not "talk." He also remembers that, when one of the other guards
began to beat him for no apparent reason, Simpson "hit him and
broke his ribs." He was later cleared of any responsibility in the
incident.

Some day, Simpson claims, he is going to write about his confinement in the mental hospital. Certainly, his six months there
somewhat soured him on America, which is understandable, especially in light of the fact that his mental condition was brought
about by the very service he gave to America, which, after the
war, at least granted him citizenship. He tells the *dust* interviewer: "Let me assure you, that place [the hospital] makes me
believe this country is a funny place because everybody is so
concerned about the wrongs that go on. But nobody knows what
goes on in a place like this." A believer in the efficacy of experience—any experience—for the writer, Simpson nevertheless sees

meaning in his six-month confinement: "But I think it's very good to see life that way."

After his release from the hospital, Simpson gradually recovered (from both his mental condition and the institution) by working days and by taking a light schedule of classes at night at the School of General Studies, Columbia University. He worked as a copyboy on the New York *Herald Tribune* and then as a packer and clerk for an import-export firm. While the jobs were menial, Simpson argues that they gave him "a sort of attitude toward the universe." He continues: "I don't take seriously some of the things my colleagues take seriously. A lot of things people consider important are less important to me. I've seen people killed, and it's given me a sort of simple gratitude for being alive." [11]

After he received a Bachelor of Science degree in 1948 from Columbia's School of General Studies, Simpson spent a year in France and, for a while, attended classes at the University of Paris. First he registered for a course in French civilization, which, he says, was "designed for Americans, especially ex-soldiers, whose dollars were needed immediately by the French." One part of the course consisted of French composition taught by an instructor whose idea of learning the language was to translate a passage from French literature into his own conception of English and then to have his students try to translate *his* English back into the original. To the poet, this class had no more value than one he took in what he calls "method," one that was taught by a "portly dame" whose own method was so strictly formal and ridiculous that Simpson says he "was reduced from an enthusiasm for French literature to stuttering, and then to silence." However, the crowning disappointment and indignity came when Simpson, after having quit the course designed for Americans, tried to register for a course about the poet Baudelaire that was designed primarily for French students. He was told that a prerequisite for admission to the course was a series of three inoculations. He took the first injection, suffered a high fever as a reaction; took the second injection, suffered with fever again; and then, understandably, decided "to give up French poetry and read the Russians in translation." [12] But his enthusiasm for French literature appears not to have been thoroughly lost, for Simpson has translated a number of works of Guillaume Apollinaire into English, including *The Breasts of Tiresias*.

V   *Back to America: The Literary Life*

During Simpson's year in France, he assembled a number of poems he had written from 1940 to 1949 into a manuscript which he published at his own expense—a practice which, beginning with Walt Whitman, has been characteristic of the first volumes of a number of major American poets. *The Arrivistes* bears the imprint of The Fine Editions Press in New York and was printed in Paris. It carried an exuberant but somewhat pedantic foreword by Theodore Hoffman. Several of the poems in *The Arrivistes* had already been published in magazines, including "Roll," which appeared in *Harper's Magazine*.

When Simpson returned to the United States, a year of supposed study in Paris and a volume of poems behind him, he married Jeanne C. Rogers, studied again at Columbia, took a Master of Arts degree in English with a thesis entitled "One Man in His Time" about John Dos Passos, and began to work in an editorial capacity for the Bobbs-Merrill Publishing Company in New York City, a job he held until 1955. In 1951, his first child, Louis Matthew Simpson was born. In 1953, he and his wife were separated and were divorced the following year. A year later, in 1955, Simpson was married to Dorothy M. Roochvarg and there are two children from this marriage: a daughter, Anne Borovoi (b. 1956), and a son, Anthony Rolfe (b. 1959). In his poetry, interviews, and essays for national magazines, the poet has said little about his immediate family, but marriage is touched upon by Simpson in a piece for *Harper's Magazine*:

> Certainly there are drawbacks to being a married writer, as there are to being a married anything. There's the house, the car, the kids shouting "Gimme!" But the unmarried writer is in no better pickle. For one thing, he will always be fretting that he is not sufficiently loved. The unmarried writer travels more, but he knows less about the ordinary lives of men and women. However, when you get down to cases, being married or unmarried does not determine the quality of a man's work. . . . What matters is the writer's intelligence.[13]

In the early 1950's, Simpson's poems began appearing with regularity in such distinguished quarterlies as the *Partisan Review*, the *American Scholar*, and the *Hudson Review*. Concurrently, he was publishing in the "little" magazines, a practice he continues. In fact, Simpson tells the *dust* interviewer that he thinks highly of the limited circulation journals, and he feels that they serve a definite purpose: to provide an outlet for developing a specific point of view. He also maintains that the readers of "little" magazines either are writers themselves or else are intensely interested in the literature of today.[14] The lack of such interest on the part of established writers, academicians, and critics in general has long disturbed Simpson. The May 29, 1954, issue of the *New Yorker* carried "Ægean," a short lyric by Simpson. Since then, he has made numerous appearances in the *New Yorker*, and in September, 1957, he entered into a first-reading contract with the magazine, which meant that the *New Yorker* had first choice on any poem Simpson wrote. Only if the *New Yorker* did not want to publish the poem was he free to submit it elsewhere. Though the poet is not convinced that the magazine has selected for publication the best of the material from him that it has received, he admits that some of his finest poems first saw print in the *New Yorker*,[15] one of which is the brilliant "My Father in the Night Commanding No." Thus Simpson's poetry has appeared in every kind of magazine, from the very limited circulation "little" magazines through the academic quarterlies and on to the big nationals.

In January, 1954, Simpson received a letter from a Robert Thomas Moore of Pasadena, California, informing the poet that he had won the first prize award of $1,250 in the annual Borestone Mountain Award competition for poetry. A week later, Moore telegraphed Simpson in New York that a "grave error occurred" in the tabulation of the judges' decisions—Simpson had not won. This error inaugurated a series of wires and letters from New York to California and back again, the gist of the matter being that the whole fouled-up affair was more than embarrassing to the contest officials (who had never erred like that before!) and a very unpleasant experience to the relatively unknown writer. When a reporter knocked at the door of the Simpson residence in Berkeley, California, in 1964 to tell the poet that his fourth collection of poems, *At the End of the Open Road*, had won a Pulitzer Prize,

Simpson did not believe it at first; for he immediately recalled the Borestone fiasco of a decade before.

Good News of Death and Other Poems was issued in 1955 in the second volume of Scribner's "Poets of Today" series. This book received more attention by the reviewers than *The Arrivistes,* and it also established Simpson as more than a competent young poet. The same year he began teaching full time at Columbia University. Two years later, as a result of his increasing stature as a poet, Simpson was appointed a *Hudson Review* Fellow in Poetry and, in addition, was awarded a Prix de Rome (a fellowship given by the American Academy of Arts and Letters). Simpson and his family spent the year 1957–58 in Rome where he wrote a doctoral dissertation, his "James Hogg, A Critical Study" (subsequently published in 1962 by Oliver & Boydin in Edinburgh and by St. Martin's Press in the United States).

When Simpson returned to New York, he continued teaching and completed all the requirements for his Doctor of Philosophy degree in comparative literature, which was awarded by Columbia in 1959. The same year Wesleyan University Press issued his third collection of poems, *A Dream of Governors,* and he moved with his family to Berkeley, California, to accept a position in the Department of English at the University of California. By this time, Simpson's reputation as a poet of significance was assured. Recognition of this fact was testified to by his nomination for a Ford Foundation Fellowship, which would have provided him a stipend for a year to be in residence with a theater company. However, Simpson replied that his commitment to the University of California made it impossible for him to be considered for the award. In 1960 the poet was the recipient of a Distinguished Service Award given by the School of General Studies, Columbia University, from which he had received a Bachelor of Science degree in 1948. This year also saw him become the winner of the Edna St. Vincent Millay Award of $200 given under the auspices of the Poetry Society of America.

Beginning in the late 1950's and continuing into the present, Simpson has given readings of his poetry at numerous colleges and universities throughout the country. He has made television appearances, and his poetry has been heard on radio broadcasts in New York, Chicago, San Francisco, London, and Rome. His poems have been recorded in the Yale series of recorded poets and elsewhere. Because of his intense commitment to writing and to his teaching responsibilities, the poet has been able to accept only about a third of the invitations he has received to read and to lecture to groups throughout the United States. However, on June 14, 1964, he did give the Sunday sermon at a Unitarian Church near his home in California: "I thought it would be fascinating for me to see what these people were like, rather than the usual academic crew. It was quite rewarding." [16]

Riverside Drive, a novel which, as I have mentioned, contains some autobiographical material, was issued in 1962 by Atheneum Publishers, and it is the fifth area of literary work in which Simpson has distinguished himself. In 1963, the poet-critic-scholar-translator-novelist was awarded a Guggenheim Fellowship, which enabled him to travel with his family through Great Britain and Italy. The same year Wesleyan University Press brought out *At the End of the Open Road,* the Pulitzer poetry selection for 1964 —the volume which has established Simpson as a major American poet.

In 1965, Harcourt, Brace & World issued Simpson's *Selected Poems,* which contains the best of his four earlier volumes and which was a contender for the National Book Award. Also in 1965 Columbia University honored its alumnus by awarding him its Medal for Excellence. In 1967, Simpson's first venture into textbook writing appeared as *Introduction to Poetry,* released by St. Martin's Press, the American publisher of *James Hogg, A Critical Study.* In the summer of 1967, Simpson left Berkeley to assume a position as Professor of English at the State University of New York, Stony Brook, Long Island, where he has remained, except for 1970–71, which he spent in London on his second Guggenheim Fellowship. In 1971, *Adventures of the Letter I,* his sixth volume of poetry, was published by Oxford University Press in London.

VI *Some Attitudes of Person*

Since 1956, except for the several years he spent in Europe on awards, Louis Simpson has taught at universities in the United States. During these years he has written most of his best poems, those which rank among the best by an American; and he has also written numerous reviews, essays on literary and nonliterary subjects, a novel, and a textbook. Though he has refrained, it appears, from incorporating directly his experiences as a teacher in his poems, he has, on several occasions, made comments in public concerning the creative writer in the academic profession: "As a writer of poems, I have had social and financial difficulties. I have tried to resolve them by earning a living as a teacher, and therefore being able to write what I want—instead of what someone else wants." [17] He tells the *dust* interviewer about the academic life, the writer, and the supposedly real world: "Most of the things said about the writer who teaches are not true. It's not that he's cut off from the real world, that he's not much in contact with, well, life. It's very funny to see a reviewer in *Time* Magazine talking about the academic poet. As if men on *Time* were in contact with reality. The danger to the academic person is that he might get a conscience. He has so many things to do that are right —but artists should be very ruthless about this. . . . You must be ruthless, and in that way antisocial." [18]

The author of "Four Who Swim Through the Desert" notes that Simpson wants to "preserve his independence as a poet." Consequently, he "shuns clubs, organizations, and cliques. And he has no desire to be a popular poet." [19] This essay, in addition, reiterates Simpson's stand on being a "good" person in the world at large. He knows, for example, that it is good to play in the yard with a child: "But I have to say to myself: I will not play with him. I don't mean I never do, but I must realize that this is a good thing to do—and this also is a good thing to do. There are so many worthwhile things in the world that an artist can do besides practice his art." [20] However, Simpson has nothing to do with either "artistic circles" or with the bohemian life, which, he argues, does not mean that he subscribes to middle-class ideas: "it is simply that I find it less distracting to live as others do than to spend my energy not to." He finds that "people who build their lives around art become ill-informed, arrogant, and stupid. On the other hand, if you move among ordinary people—and not as a stranger, but subject to the things they feel—you can learn much." Thus Simpson, who continues to attack in his poetry many of the concepts for which the American middle-class has come to stand, finds that in ordinary life there is much material worth writing about:

"There is material in everyday life for poetry that will be neither esoteric nor banal. Except in Whitman and Hart Crane we have had very little of this poetry in America. We do not find in writing[,] images that correspond to the lives we really have." [21]

CHAPTER 2

The Arrivistes

T HE *Arrivistes,* Simpson's first volume of poetry, contains thirty lyrics and two verse plays—*The Vagrants* and the title piece—all of which were written between 1940 and 1949. The critical consensus of reviewers of Simpson's first book is generally favorable, but there are some reservations. Writing in the October 1, 1949, issue of the *Nation,* Rolfe Humphries cites the skill with which the poet manages "quite a variety of forms." The distinguished British critic David Daiches, in January 8, 1950, in the New York *Herald Tribune Book Week,* was to be proven wrong later in his original contention that there is "not a single poem of sustained effectiveness in *The Arrivistes.*" One of the most amusing notices appeared in the *Gleaner* (Kingston, Jamaica) for October 27, 1949. In the review, A. L. Hendrick evinced irritation because of Simpson's dark view of the world and also gave Simpson advice: "I suggest that Louis Simpson should come home for a while that his talent may be re-infused with the light of these islands before it is infected further by the despondence of Europe and the brittle brashness of North America."

I *War*

Approximately a third of the lyrics included in *The Arrivistes,* excluding the verse plays, deal either directly or indirectly with war. The most impressive of these are "Arm in Arm," "Carentan O Carentan," "Resistance," and "Roll"; the first two poems concern actual combat; the last two, the aftermath of combat. "Arm in Arm," Theodore Hoffman enthusiastically tells us in his Preface to *The Arrivistes,* is a "poem in which war, at its most devastating and meaningful moment, is taken as a stunned, airless landscape in which figures are breathless and voiceless, and the underlying

terror of uncertainty is hinted at only by lines that end successfully a foot short of expectation and a penultimate stanza that runs
an instant over."

"Arm in Arm" is the poetized version of Simpson's combat encounter in the graveyard at Verghel, Holland. The setting of a
graveyard provides him with an inherent irony of which he makes
good use in the poem itself. The speaker is a soldier, undoubtedly
Simpson himself, as he seems to be in most of his poems unless we
are told otherwise. The situation of the poem is the shelling of
infantry soldiers and the omnipresence of the death that inexorably accompanies combat. As is fairly typical in most of Simpson's
war poems, he has his speaker relate the circumstances in a rather
flip, singsong fashion. The twenty-four lines, forming six quatrains,
are rhymed *abab* in alternating iambic tetrameter and trimeter.
Yohma Gray, the critic, argues that the "fragmentary senselessness
of the experience is enhanced by the deliberately measured and
regular meter." [1] The fact that the soldiers are naïvely approach-
ing combat arm in arm brings to mind a scene of children as they
are being led by the teacher to a playground, an implied parallel
providing a structural unity throughout the poem. The speaker is
an innocent who, while obviously involved in the thick of battle,
seems nevertheless detached; his pose creates a bitterness that is
ironic in nature.

"Arm in Arm" begins, in fact, with a sense of the make-believe:

> Arm in arm in the Dutch dyke
> Were piled both friend and foe
> With rifle, helmet, motor-bike:
> Step over as you go.

Easily, the third line could be altered to read "bat, ball, bicycle,"
or the like. As the soldiers moved in columns toward the graveyard where they were shelled by the enemy in a surprise assault,
they came across the captain, whose head was being held by a
"little Dutch girl" who was in the act of giving him "a jug of milk/
In which his blood did run." The inclusion of a child in the poem
suggests the gamelike quality of the situation. The dying captain,
a symbol of adult leadership, was unable to warn his charges of
the impending attack. Thus the children-soldiers in the graveyard
were forced to dig foxholes that were "too shallow for our souls/
When the ground began to toss."

The method by which the poet relates the innocents' reactions to the shelling is, in itself, so open-eyed and incredible that the concluding quatrains of the poem are perfectly appropriate and, at the same time, functionally ambiguous:

> Which were the new, which the old dead
> It was a sight to ask.
> One private found a polished head
> And took the skull to task
>
> For spying on us. . . . Till along
> Driving the clouds like sheep,
> Our bombers came in a great throng:
> And so we fell asleep.

Miss Gray feels that the "strife of the battle is heightened by the suggestion of sleep and of the calm of the pastoral scene." [2] There is certainly a heightening, but it seems rather to be the natural culmination of the play-soldiers' activities. The confusion between what is terribly real and what is make-believe is underscored both by the soldiers' inability to distinguish their own corpses from those already entombed and by the private's taking a skull to task for spying; both acts are as absurd as the act of war itself is to the speaker of the poem. The allusions to sheep in the last stanza and the coming of bombers "in a great throng" serve once more to exemplify the parallel between children and soldiers; both need to be led, and both are incapable, for the most part, of specific kinds of understanding. Falling asleep may be construed as a form of escapism, as it often is for children; but in the poem it could mean, in addition, the death of the soldiers, ironically by their own bombs, were it not for the nagging reality that the speaker is *remembering* this initiation to combat, though the dreamlike quality of his memory suggests that he could already be dead. Simpson is also suggesting the universality of war by not identifying on whose side the soldiers in question fought. To anyone, war is bad.

The same quality of bewildered innocence marks Simpson's most successful war poem, "Carentan O Carentan," but the speaker's presence in this poem is more clearly focused and felt than in "Arm in Arm." Both poems use a similar ballad technique, with alternating iambic tetrameter and trimeter lines and with a simple *abab* rhyme pattern. The basic situations of both poems are similar: a surprise attack by the enemy on soldiers who were un-initiated into the ways of combat and death. In "Carentan O Carentan," Simpson more carefully depicts the scene just before the surprise attack, which in this case is an infantry ambush rather than an artillery shelling. The opening quatrain tells of a pastoral scene replete with lovers:

> Trees in the old days used to stand
> And shape a shady lane
> Where lovers wandered hand in hand
> Who came from Carentan.

The use of the past tense in these lines forbodes the ominous, which is also prefigured in the last line of the second quatrain in which the speaker, after telling of the soldiers walking two by two in "combat-interval" along a "shining green canal," talks of "Such trees we never knew"—trees in which the enemy waited in concealment for the right moment to ambush the inexperienced platoon. To communicate the sense of utter peace so anachro-nistic to war, and thus a means by which tension is created in the poem, the speaker addresses the reader directly in lines that ring of Robert Frost:

> Could you have seen us through a glass
> You would have said a walk
> Of farmers out to turn the grass,
> Each with his own hay-fork.

But the enemy, camouflaged in leopard skins, was doing the ac-tual looking.

The speaker then moves from the "we" to the "I" point of view, personalizing the immediacy of combat, which he could not do through consistent use of the collective point of view used in "Arm in Arm." In the seventh quatrain, he tells of a "hammer at my knee," which he knows must make him "lie down at once" and which he labels as either "death or cowardice." All he is certain of is: "Don't count again on me."

The qualities of innocence and of childlike need for authority, which so distinguish "Arm in Arm," become the tonal determi-nants in "Carentan O Carentan" from the seventh to the concluding quatrain. First, the speaker assures his mother that "Everything's all right," for "Everyone gets the same/ At one time or another./ It's all in the game." Second, as if denying the entire experience, or blotting it, so to speak, right out of his mind and yet acknowledging it at the same time, the speaker confides to his mother:

> I never strolled, nor ever shall,
> Down such a leafy lane.
> I never drank in a canal,
> Nor ever shall again.

The confusion between what is and what is not real is similar to that which exists in a child's mind after he has done something wrong, something of which he knows his mother would not approve.

Three symbols of authority fallen in combat provide the subjects for quatrains eleven through thirteen. First, the speaker turns for help to the master sergeant, then to the captain, and finally to the lieutenant; but each is dead, and each is described as if the speaker were a child unable to comprehend fully that the authority can no longer tell him what to do. The master sergeant is "silent/ That taught me how to do it"; the "Captain's sickly/ And taking a long nap"; and the lieutenant is "a sleeping beauty,/ Charmed by that strange tune." The immediacy of war is heightened in the second half of the poem through a change in tense from past to present. "Carentan O Carentan" concludes with a mature but simply stated evaluation of the speaker's reaction to the ambush:

> Carentan O Carentan
> Before we met with you
> We never yet had lost a man
> Or known what death could do.

When this poem appeared in *The Arrivistes*, it was ignored by the reviewers; but it has since been highly acclaimed. For example, the reviewer in the November 1, 1963, issue of the London *Times Literary Supplement* says: "'Carentan O Carentan' is a fine achievement: a combat poem which is clear, understated in a ballad technique and humanely ironic." He has more praise to offer in the June 9, 1966, issue: "'Carentan O Carentan' is an early war poem that gradually accumulates menace yet proceeds with all the grace of a minuet. . . . The mode involves the directness and simplicity of a ballad structure and a cavalier fastidiousness about diction." Robert Bly, who has followed Simpson's literary career with great interest, writes in 1958 that "Carentan O Carentan" is the "best poem written yet about World War II by any generation." [3] And C. B. Cox writes in 1966 that it is "perhaps his best war poem." [4] Despite the obvious value of the poem and its slow but eventual recognition, Simpson in 1964 tells the *dust* interviewer of his dissatisfaction: "It has taken all these years for some one to read that poem. . . . Now I can't be much interested in that poem. What you are doing now deals with the moment and you can lose interest, move on to other things by the time people read your work." [5]

In terms of technique, "Carentan O Carentan" is exemplary of Simpson's ability in his early years to write extremely successful lyrics. The alternating metrics provide the balladlike way of depicting a situation so real that it is archetypal. Point of view alternates from the collective to the personal, both universalizing and personalizing the experience. Tension is created through the seeming disparity of form and subject matter, which is not so much a disparity as a perfect union of the innocent and the terrible. The contrast of the bucolic with the leopard ambush adds another tension. Even the rhymes are flawless, with both near and perfect interchanged. One of the technical successes is simply that the poet has created meaning through form; and, wherever the threat of technical dominance impinges—as it always does in a poem employing rhyme—Simpson substitutes similar sounds, giving us, for example, the near rhymes of "suits"—"boot," "leaves"—"knives," and "wind—ground." The other achievements of "Carentan O Carentan" are many, but they have already been discussed.

In both "Roll" and "Resistance," Simpson departs from the ballad textures of "Arm in Arm" and "Carentan O Carentan" in order to use deliberately rough metrics. The setting of both is after the war; the speaker of both is questioning the values that war forces men to adopt. "Roll" begins dramatically and curiously: "What, my friends! Dead only two years and already dumb?/ Must we hang your skulls in the square?/ You've acres enough. Move over and give us your graves." This acidity takes us off guard; but, when we read on, we find it continues into the second stanza, climaxing in a line so bitter that it, at first, seems totally inappropriate and, in fact, profane: "Here rentals are rising: how is it in your neighborhood?" The last three stanzas of the poem justify the speaker's outrage, the product of his dual feelings of confusion and helplessness. The soldiers who died on the beachhead in the invasion of Normandy have died for reasons incomprehensible to the speaker. He finds it impossible to make any sense from the war; and, as a soldier himself, he is unable to do anything to alter the events of war.

In "Roll," the men are referred to as "dumb," "silent," and "skeleton stoics" because the speaker is unable to think of them as having any identities. Since their deaths have given no knowledge to the speaker, they must be considered as meaningless. Then the speaker wonders if in their graves the soldiers will metaphorically rise to the "roll": "They call to the companies: will you rise to the roll. . ./ To Russia, wherever, laughing/ Again to be marching, again to be going to war?" He remembers one of the dying soldiers asking, "Why am I here?" The speaker "would bring him a wreath," but fear rouses the soldier's wrath. The poem concludes with the speaker's honest confession that still, two years after Utah Beach, he can offer no knowledge of why men must fight and die: "I'd say more, but my tongue is no trumpet."

"Roll" is a protest poem that expresses Simpson's antiwar attitude, an attitude germane to an understanding of his poems to come out of his involvement in World War II. As Miss Gray has stated, "Simpson is an intellectually mature and responsible poet who is ultimately committed to making human sense of what *is*, although he is never unaware of the eternal paradoxes and possibilities of what *ought to be*. His war poems, for example, intensify particulars but ominously suggest also in a systematic way that war is a singularly ineffective behavior pattern if the human animal really wants to improve his condition." [6] "Roll" also contrasts the romantic notions of war that soldiers may hold before combat and the dedication to roll inculcated into them with the actual fact of death that they must confront and to which some must succumb. Obviously, the speaker feels he is in no better position than the dead soldiers, were they able to speak, for he enjoins them to "Move over and give us [the living] your graves." There is no glory, glamor, and little sense to war, an attitude Simpson makes continual use of in both his poetry and prose.

Though he sees little to admire in war as an entity, Simpson recognizes that there are people and acts in whom honor and bravery exist. One such person is Jean Gardère of the French *résistance*, a man who was "cowardly slain" and for whom a cross and photograph mark his grave on "the winding road under the white Alp." "Resistance," an experiment in colloquialism, is primarily about the values in, and the purpose of, war and about postwar attitudes toward a specific aspect of the war. "Resistance" is a better poem than "Roll"; the latter relies too heavily on the speaker's shocking his readers into attention, and it is also put together rather disjointedly. "Resistance" presents a complete, unified experience; and the poem concludes with, what Randall Jarrell calls in an undated letter to Simpson, an "extremely moving" passage.

The time of "Resistance" is three years after the war; the setting is the spot in the Alps, now a ski slope, where the memorial to Jean Gardère has been erected. After these facts have been established, the speaker begins a series of questions to Jean Gardère himself, one of which asks if the patriot was shot or bayoneted in the back, and another is "How did you resist/ The actual unimagined agony?" This question repeats what Simpson often suggests in his war poems: that those involved in the actual fighting are unprepared for the reality of facing death. Here the adjective "unimagined" carries the point. Since Jean Gardère was not in the military as such, the speaker questions why he became involved in the first place. Perhaps, the speaker speculates, a "German stole your cow"; or perhaps "you'd read Rimbaud when you were twelve"; or perhaps "your papers [were] slightly out of order"; or perhaps "you cherish[ed] the tricolor, which, in a ribbon,/ Decorates your darkening photograph?" No answers are forthcoming, of course, yet the speaker remarks bitterly, which is reminiscent of the opening of "Roll," "That's what the dead are for, to answer questions."

The first five stanzas, then, set the ground for the last five, in which the speaker tries to find meaning in Jean Gardère's participation in the *résistance* and in his subsequent death. He does

so through a complex series of contrasts based on the colors of
the French flag; through the red, white, and blue of the skiers'
outfits as the "skiers go laughing/ To the sun-struck slopes";
through the white color of the snow; and finally through the
voice of the wind which "says/ Resisters are somewhat silly." The
point of stanzas six through eight seems to be that, now that the
war is over, the whole unpleasant business has been conveniently
forgotten, fun has been restored, and the patriot's memorial has
become, in effect, no more than an obstacle to the skiers. In the
fallen snow, which is "the international/ Color, which all our lives
in a perfect world/ Would have, and souls in heaven too," Jean
Gardère's "scarlet flow is neither here nor there." But it is not
right, the speaker contends, to dismiss the national hero in terms
that both the skiers (society) and the snow and wind (nature)
would. The speaker probes further: "You felt perhaps the gesture
to be out-dated/ As a boy's dream, a story of knights in armor."
Whatever it was that prompted Jean Gardère to fight for the
résistance, the speaker concludes,

> Nevertheless, you made it in slow motion
>
> On the frozen surface of the stony road,
> Your feeble flurry of resistance,
> That you, not the living, might seem out of place.

It is inevitable that the poem must end here, for the speaker is
too aware of the irony that the hero is regarded by both society
and nature as an anachronism to continue.

II *Love*

"Carentan O Carentan" (there are others as well) certainly
disproves the claims in reviews by both David Daiches and Randell Jarrell that, as Daiches puts it, there is "not a single poem
of sustained effectiveness" in *The Arrivistes*. The only known reviewer to notice and to praise, at least in part, "Carentan O
Carentan" is Mark Reinsberg in *Voices* (Spring, 1950). Jarrell,
in the February, 1950, issue of *Poetry Unlimited*, is rather comprehensive in his over-all assessment of the volume: "There isn't
a good poem in *The Arrivistes*, but Louis Simpson is as promising

a new poet as I've read in some time. His poems are gay, felt, mocking, rather inexperienced, thoroughly uneven, thoroughly unexpected poems; they are not organized or thought out into successful works of art, but a few of their lines or stanzas are good, and more than a few are beautifully funny . . . at his best he is witty and moving, a fine amateur who ought—with luck—to turn into a good professional."

The war poems are not witty, clever, gay, or humorous, but they are indeed moving and ironic. The other qualities, including irony, abound in the love poems, which, like the war poems, constitute about a third of the lyrics in *The Arrivistes*. In these love poems, Simpson resorts at times to inversions and to other archaic conventions in order to achieve rhyme. He often sounds, in fact, like an Elizabethan song-maker or like a Cavalier poet. Several of the love poems succeed better than others in infusing modern situations with the standard techniques of some time ago.

In "A Witty War," a good poem with which to begin an analysis, the speaker is a man who has gone through a trial by wit that "flourished seven years" with a woman who had "jetty shining hair" and brown eyes. The poem consists of four stanzas of six lines of iambic pentameter; each stanza follows the same *ababaa* rhyme pattern, with the words *knows* and *care* providing the bases for the two rhymes for the entire poem. Inversions are employed at least twice, perhaps more, depending upon how much the reader is willing to accept as natural. In any event, the relationship between the man and woman was founded, or so the speaker is trying to ascertain, on purely physical grounds. Apparently the lovers, in good Cavalier fashion, engaged in a constant series of repartees, which in turn led to "kisses," which in turn led to "cares" (note the pun here), all of which led finally each time to disrobing and then: "Oh, we loved long and happily, God knows!" At least for seven years, for inevitably a "silent treason" grew, eyes met each other emptily, or else filled with tears; and the "tender greenness" of the lovers vanished. "A Witty War" concludes with the lovers separated, apparently forever, and with the man philosophizing: "This nakedness is all our own, God knows,/ And shall remain till time makes us some clothes,"— their spiritual nakedness will last until the man and woman, or perhaps boy and girl, mature emotionally. There is not much substance to this poem, though it is clever, witty, technically sound,

and ends ironically. "A Witty War" is, I think, the kind of poem
for which now Simpson would have little use; and to this statement we find some testimony in the fact that he revised the poem
for its inclusion in *A Dream of Governors* ten years later in 1959.

The first significant change is in the new title, "The Custom of
the World." The title phrase appears in the new concluding line
of the poem; "The custom of the world is wearing clothes" re-
places "And shall remain till time makes us some clothes." The
thematic consideration in the new version is altered from time
someday bringing emotional maturity to the lovers to society
frowning on the nefarious sexual play of the man and, as he now
refers to the woman, his mistress.

There are other changes as well. The whole conception of a
repartee of wit, from which the original title is taken, has been
omitted from "The Custom of the World." For example, these
lines from "A Witty War,"

> A witty war that flourished seven years,
> Where the small river to the ocean flows.
> Our quarrel made us kiss, kisses brought cares,
> And closeness caused the taking off of clothes.

become in "The Custom of the World":

> The ocean danced, the green leaves tossed, the air
> Was filled with petals, and pale Venus rose
> When we began to kiss. Kisses brought care,
> And closeness caused the taking off of clothes.

The "silent treason" is still there, but it takes on a different dimension in "The Custom of the World." The focus is altered from
a seven-year interlude in "A Witty War" to an impulsive one-
night affair in the second version, though the sexual behavior of
the man and woman still carries the blame. In "A Witty War," we
are led to believe that the lovers will never meet again, but we
are told by the speaker of "The Custom of the World" that "when
we meet again let us suppose/ We never loved or ever naked
were."

Through the speaker's awareness of the unacceptable sexual
behavior of his mistress and himself, at least insofar as society is
concerned, he becomes the man for whom time in the first version

would someday make clothes. "The Custom of the World" is both
a tightened and, at the same time, expanded version of "A Witty
War": tightened, in that a specific incident is made to carry significance; expanded, in that the closing line is an ironic indictment of a society in which wearing clothes rather than being
people has become the "custom of the world." Even though the
second version looks the same in form—same meter, stanza divisions, and essentially the same rhymes—the quality of the writing
is superior. Lines which seemed rhythmically awkward are now
smoother; images are sharper and more functional.

The most interesting and perhaps the best love lyric in *The
Arrivistes* is "Song: 'Rough Winds Do Shake the Darling Buds of
May.'" Like "Carentan O Carentan," the poem appears in two
subsequent volumes of Simpson's poetry: *A Dream of Governors*
and *Selected Poems*. In *A Dream of Governors*, the poem carries
the abbreviated title "Rough Winds Do Shake," but in *Selected
Poems*, the title is restored to its original length. The poem has
undergone only one change in its two later printings: the inclusion of a comma after the word *Well* in the fourth stanza. The
title is taken from the third line of Shakespeare's Sonnet XVIII.
Rhythmically, "Song: 'Rough Winds Do Shake the Darling Buds
of May'" is a fascinating and successful experiment, with lines
placed in topographical patterns rather than conventionally. The
poem celebrates the sexual eagerness of a sixteen-year-old girl
whose need is satisfied by

<blockquote>

one come to joust

Who has a horn

       sweet horn,

           and spear to sink

Before he rests.

</blockquote>

The girl of this poem seems to be Mona, the sensually exciting
and excited girl of Simpson's novel, *Riverside Drive*. The relationship of Mona and Duncan, the protagonist, may indeed be a fictionalized version of "A Witty War."

"Summer Storm," perhaps yet another Mona-Duncan poem, has
also been reprinted in *A Dream of Governors* and in *Selected
Poems*. A modern love poem, it is set in a city park and concerns
the sexual play of a young man and woman. Society is again the
enemy, this time appearing in the form of a lady who "coming on

them in the dark/ In a white fixture, wrote to the newspapers/
Complaining of the statues in the park." The speaker, an observer
outside the events of the poem, does not condemn the lovers for
their nocturnal behavior in the park, which also was enacted, we
learn from the first stanza, in other places as well:

> In that so sudden summer storm they tried
> Each bed, couch, closet, carpet, car-seat, table,
> Both river banks, five fields, a mountain side,
> Covering as much ground as they were able.

The summer storm, a metaphor for intense physical attraction, is
so furious that not only the lady in the park felt its passion:

> The envious oxen in still rings would stand
> Ruminating. Their sweet incessant plows
> I think had changed the contours of the land
> And made two modest conies move their house.

In this Shakespearian sonnet, we can accept the lady, rabbits,
and contours of the land being changed by the metaphorical
"sweet incessant plows," but we are hard put to accept the "en-
vious oxen," who surely would be as out of place in a park as the
concerned citizen thinks the lovers are. But, to give Simpson his
due, he does use the conditional "would stand" to describe the
oxen "Ruminating." And perhaps the oxen belong in one of the
"five fields," though this reading, a logical one, does not seem to
fit in with Simpson's intention. At any rate, everyone can rest, for
now the lovers are married and "Nature breathes once more."

III The City

"Invitation to a Quiet Life," another lyric, succeeds, according
to Milton Cane in the February 19, 1950, *New York Times Book
Review*, by "maintaining within its frame a delightful unity of
tone and diction which is neither wholly seventeenth century
nor wholly twentieth century." That is, "Invitation to a Quiet
Life," set in New York City in the present, is in the form of a
Renaissance song, "an ironic rewriting of a pastoral by Andrew
Marvell or Robert Herrick." In seven stanzas, each with five
iambic tetrameter couplets, the speaker, who is addressing "Ama-

ryllis," his love, sings of the city's middle-class mediocrity, its conformity, and, at the same time, of his and Amaryllis' commitment to this very way of life. Herein lies the basic irony from which the wit of the poem is loosed.

The speaker and Amaryllis are about to go to a movie theater where, it appears, everyone in America wants to go in order to "applaud/ The ecstasies we can't afford." But first, the lovers must take a taxi to Times Square:

> But first [let us], flock to the seasonal
>
> Sheep-shearing in the Great White Way
> Where thousands sacrifice their pay
> In groves to oracles, and pass
> Gazing at goddesses in glass.
> Here every Beauty on parade
> Compares the compromise she's made,
> And former school-friends when they meet
> Look down and fidget on their feet.
> Then, Amaryllis, we shall be
> Equal to our society.

This is good, wittily ironic writing; but it is also young writing in that this is how a clever young man describes and interprets the glittering façade of the Big City. The surface descriptions are done well, but the perceptions carry no insights as they do in Louis Simpson's later poems. There is little need to discuss further "Invitation to a Quiet Life," for what it sets out to do, it succeeds in doing; but its successes do not sustain us for long. The poem does, however, hold interest because of its concern with the city, a topic that has been fairly consistent with Simpson since his earliest efforts at writing poetry but one that recently is beginning to lose a hold on him: "I think a lot of poetry of the last twenty years [since World War II] has been city poetry, but a lot of it is moving out away in people like myself." [7]

Roughly a sonnet, "Room and Board" expresses the alienation of people who live in New York City in boardinghouses. Its language is understated and colloquial. Written in 1948, "Room and Board" antedates by ten years or more Simpson's poems in the "natural voice of man," and it is, therefore, of special interest. It also deserves our attention for its noticeable lack of wit and

irony that mark most of his early poems. Its despair comes
through without the need to shock and without either bitterness
or exaggerated sentiment:

> The curtained windows of New York
> Conceal her secrets. Walls of stone
> Muffle the clatter of the fork.
> Tomorrow we shall see the bone.
>
> In silence we construct a sect . . .
> Each of us, comrades, has his own.
> Poems that will not take effect,
> Pictures that never will be known.
>
> The landlord wipes his mouth of pork,
> Pauses to eavesdrop, disconnects
> The water and the telephone;
>
> And Death's unmarried daughter crawls
> Along the thin lath of the walls
> And knocks, because we live alone.

"Laertes in Paris" is a seven-part, rhymed poem that fits exclusively into none of the categories of war, love, and the city;
but it touches on each of these subjects. Rather, "Laertes in
Paris" is an intense, introspective lyric about man's need to confront eventually the responsibilities that living exacts. The point
of view is direct address by the speaker to Laertes, who stands
in this poem for the archetypal man who prefers romantic escape
to confrontations. Shakespeare's character thus serves as name
and as somewhat of a model for Simpson's protagonist, who, it
seems likely to assume, is Simpson himself. The poet felt that
his year-long interlude in Paris (1948) was something of an escape—a means by which he could postpone thinking about what
he was to do with his life. "Laertes in Paris" was finished by
Simpson in January, 1949, close to the time he returned to New
York from Paris.

For Laertes in the poem, the city of Paris serves as Lethe, the
river of forgetfulness, a place where he can indulge himself to
the extent that he is able to erase thoughts of responsibility.
He loves and is loved in return by a pretty, black-haired girl,

but she fails to provide what he is looking for: "so much sweetness sets your teeth on edge." He skips classes at the Sorbonne, then takes up with a dancing girl, "Letting her jewels trickle" through his hands; eventually he comes to learn that this life, if it is allowed to continue, "means disgrace." Then the letter arrives, telling the protagonist of his father's death and his sister's madness. Shakespeare's Laertes had to return to Denmark, just as the Laertes of this poem must come to terms with himself. The closing section of the poem contains both the theme and the most impressive writing:

> Each man has his Hamlet, that dark other
> Self who is the conscience left behind,
> Who should be cherished dearly as a brother
> But is a sort of madness of the mind:
> A serious dark-dressed entire shape
> From which no slightest duty can escape.
>
> And every man his Denmark, that dark country,
> Familiar, incestuous, to which
> He must return, in his turn to stand sentry
> Until his blood has filled the Castle ditch,
> And clear his father's honor with his life,
> And take a perfect ignorance to wife.
>
> To Denmark, then. To face the breaking storm,
> The ghosts, the duty, the ingratitude.
> God knows you wished that thinking man no harm
> And Paris seemed a lasting interlude.
> But that the stream of life may be renewed
> One man must die, the other may sleep warm.

Louis Simpson returned to New York, where he continued with increasing success the serious business of a serious poet—the writing and publishing of poems.

CHAPTER *3*

Good News of Death

IN a letter dated November 18, 1954, when John Hall Wheelock, then editor of Scribner's "Poets of Today" series, informed Louis Simpson that *Good News of Death and Other Poems* was selected for inclusion in the second volume of the series, he wrote Simpson: "There is fine work in these poems, and we shall be proud to add them to the Scribner list." Before the collection appeared, Donald Hall prophesied the success that *Good News of Death and Other Poems* was to meet: "It will probably be the best book of the year. He has immense powers of stylistic variation, from the ballad swing of 'The Ash and the Oak,' through the quiet exactness of 'The Battle,' the triple meters of 'The Heroes,' and the pure lyricism of 'Song.' . . . Perhaps Simpson will be the poet of the Second World War; it is a consistent subject." [1] And two months before publication, in a letter of July 25, 1955, Mark Van Doren wrote Simpson: "*Good News of Death* is better than ever. I mean the whole collection, though I mean the pastoral too. You have a wonderful wit that never, I swear, stops playing. It is the seed of your seriousness, but meanwhile a joy forever; and so I know you will always be a fine poet, however many changes you go through."

In addition to the poems of Simpson, Scribner's *Poets of Today II* contains the work of two other poets: *The Hatch*, by Norma Farber, and *The Irony of Joy*, by Robert Pack. The volume is prefaced by "Introductory Essay: The Fourth Voice of Poetry" by John Hall Wheelock, in which Simpson is quoted as saying of the poems composing *Good News of Death and Other Poems*:

These poems are parts of my life. I have, like most men, made journeys, and have loved; like most men of my generation, I have seen or heard of wars. I do not apologize in these poems for my own experience, nor do I feel these things have been said before.

Indeed, as they happened to me, they have never before been said
by anyone. That is why I have written the poems. I have kept
the lines clean of words and references that have to be looked up.
Each poem explains itself. No Chinese, no footnotes. In "Good
News of Death" [the twelve page title piece] I have even taken
care to tell who Orestes was, at the risk of telling the scholar what
he already knows. The poems were not written for scholars, but
for common people. I once thought of calling them Lyric and
Dramatic Poems. They are lyric in manner: the sound is the form—
the sound gives a dimension of feeling. Dramatic: because the
poems deal, more or less, with a Dramatic or human situation,
as opposed to metaphysics, literature or a transitory mood.

Reviewers were enthusiastic about *Good News of Death and
Other Poems.* Among those who found much to admire in the col-
lection were John Ciardi (*New York Times Book Review,* August
14, 1955), Randell Jarrell (*Harper's Magazine,* October, 1955),
Phillip Booth (*Village Voice,* November 23, 1955), Edwin Honig
(*Partisan Review,* Winter, 1956), Hazard Adams (*American
Scholar,* Spring, 1956), Donald Hall (*New Orleans Poetry Journal,* April, 1956), and Mona Van Duyn (*Poetry,* August, 1956).
Miss Van Duyn best summarizes the qualities reviewers singled
out for mention: "These are suave and polished poems, very fine
ones. One would have to search hard to find any stumbling in
metrics or imagery. To describe them, one thinks of such terms
as intellectual, witty, understated."

She is right; for, where Simpson at times sounds awkward in
The Arrivistes, he is indeed polished in poems of the new col-
lection. His firm rhythms strike insistently; there is little straining
for rhyme; and, in a few of the poems, he works with the natural
qualities of a colloquial language that eventually distinguishes
Simpson's later poems, notably those dating from and included in
At the End of the Open Road (1963). Simpson's commitments in
Good News of Death and Other Poems are to the formal traditions of English poetry, at least in technical matters. By 1955,
Simpson had developed into the "good professional" that Randell
Jarrell had predicted in his review of *The Arrivistes.* This very
commitment to the conventions disturbed Robert Bly, who wrote
in 1958 that Simpson should "search for a form as fresh as his
content." [2] But "American Preludes" and "West," which are dis-

cussed later in this chapter, specifically prefigure the new direction Bly seemed to want.

In *Good News of Death and Other Poems*, Simpson proves that he is superb as a technician, but this statement should not be taken to mean that his successes are only technical. Both images and rhythms are handled so effectively that they contribute to intensity and meaning. There is also a wider variety of subjects than in the first volume, including poems dealing with the American continent and poems built from classical situations; but Simpson continues to write about war and love—the two major subject divisions of his first collection.

I *War*

The four war poems in *Good News of Death and Other Poems* reinforce the contention that Louis Simpson is a major literary interpreter in America of World War II. Each war poem is formal in that it follows the conventions of meter, rhyme, and stanza arrangements, and each blends successfully the "natural voice of man" into a pre-established format. "Memories of a Lost War" consists of six stanzas, the metrics alternating between lines of iambic pentameter and dimeter, and the rhyme scheme is a standard *abab*. The alternating metrics contribute to the singsong quality consistent with the childlike comprehension that Simpson frequently works into his war lyrics. Through the use of the collective "we," the speaker identifies himself as one of the infantry soldiers; but he acts, in addition, as an outside observer in the last two stanzas by addressing the soldiers as "you" and "they."

The poem begins by establishing that the foot soldiers march in "fearful file" in contrast to the factual surety of guns that know "what is what." Like "Arm in Arm" and "Carentan O Carentan," the two poems from *The Arrivistes* dealing explicitly with the infantry, "Memories of a Lost War" stresses the manner in which the men march into combat. This factor is important since the filing of the men—"arm in arm," "in combat-interval"—must suggest to the poet the affinities infantry soldiers share with children. Then, as in both of the earlier poems, the enemy opens fire, catching the soldiers off guard in a surprise maneuver. The ambush is described in the second stanza, beginning with an excellent simile, followed by factual understatement:

> The scene jags like a strip of celluloid.
> A mortar fires,
> Cinzano falls, Michelin is destroyed,
> The man of tires.

There is no single incident that serves as an ordering device for the poem; the structure is developed by descriptions of combat and by the lulls between. The images are made to carry the weight of perception, and they do so with great effect, as in the fourth stanza in the image of sleep:

> Hot lightnings stitch the blind eye of the moon,
> The thunder's blunt.
> We sleep. Our dreams pass in a faint platoon
> Toward the front.

But sleep can offer only temporary escape from combat. In the fifth stanza, the speaker, changing his point of view, directly addresses the soldiers as if they were children:

> Sleep well, for you are young. Each tree and bush
> Drips with sweet dew,
> And earlier than morning June's cool hush
> Will waken you.

This description brings to mind the third quatrain of "Carentan O Carentan":

> The day was early June, the ground
> Was soft and bright with dew.
> Far away the guns did sound,
> But here the sky was blue.

And, when morning does come to the soldiers of "Memories of a Lost War,"

> The riflemen will wake and hold their breath.
> Though they may bleed
> They will be proud a while of something death
> Still seems to need.

By shifting from the collective point of view to direct address and finally to the third person, the speaker has extricated himself from involvement and becomes the poet Louis Simpson affirming the dignity and the strong desire to live of the riflemen, who, like pawns in a game over which they assert no authority, do hold nevertheless to something of value—themselves—which, it must seem to Simpson, war does everything in its power to deny. Though "Memories of a Lost War" is formally constructed, the colloquial diction and rhythms, along with fresh perceptions through images, anticipate Simpson's later poems in which all formalities are abandoned in favor of a method based upon the Surrealistic deep image.

"The Battle," which is based on an incident recorded in *Riverside Drive*, possesses qualities and a theme similar to those found in "Memories of a Lost War"; but the innocence of the soldiers is replaced by a maturity that comes from continual exposure to combat. It is a sober poem in which the speaker talks in the opening stanzas as if he were an outside observer but who, in the fourth and final stanza, tells us that he too was there. In terms of point of view, "The Battle" is developed in just the opposite way from "Memories of a Lost War."

"The Battle" is a straightforward, hard-nosed account of the 101st Airborne's defense of Bastogne. The poem begins typically for Simpson with an account of the soldiers marching; again there is no suggestion of innocence:

> Helmet and rifle, pack and overcoat
> Marched through a forest. Somewhere up ahead
> Guns thudded. Like the circle of a throat
> The night on every side was turning red.

The image of the night is particularly impressive and demonstrates how far in image making ability Simpson has come since *The Arrivistes*.

By introducing the "I" point of view and by focusing in on the personal qualities of the soldiers, the closing stanza is a moving affirmation of their need and of their human right to survive:

> Most clearly of that battle I remember
> The tiredness in eyes, how hands looked thin
> Around a cigarette, and the bright ember
> Would pulse with all the life there was within.

Since the speaker, one whose life pulsed in the "bright ember," survived and now can look back, some years removed from the battle, he is able to move from a strictly sober to a more relaxed posture, which is, in fact, demanded since he now talks of the soldiers in human rather than in the mechanical terms of the first three stanzas.

The English poet and critic Thom Gunn has remarked about effectiveness of "The Battle":

> I know of almost no other poem about war which, soberly, without either hysteria or irony, is as convincing. The first three stanzas are factual—a description of things as they are—but the metaphors are already working to prepare us for the end: the soldiers have become things, or passive animals. The feeling, which is considerable, is delayed until the last stanza . . . and is then carefully revealed by the double reference of the word "within" but at the same time controlled by the use of an apparently impersonal image which leads naturally from the scene described. The point to be made is that such control does not take from the feeling—it adds to it.[3]

If I correctly understand Gunn, he is arguing that Simpson is presenting us with a view that the soldiers have been reduced from men to impersonal referents and that the poet has reinforced this belief in the last stanza by the image of the burning tip of a cigarette. Gunn believes, as well, that the impersonal, controlling image adds to the feeling of the soldiers' having been depersonalized by war. Though Gunn recognizes the basic attitude of the poem as one of sympathy, he seems to miss the point that humanity asserts its dignity to fight against the seemingly overwhelming force of war.

In "The Ash and the Oak," Simpson reverts to wit and irony to counter the belief that modern war can offer any glamor to the infantry soldier. Simpson also suggests that historically war has never been a legitimate entity. There were, it appears, at least some mitigating qualities in war as it was early practiced by the foot soldier. These are totally absent, however, in modern war, represented in this poem by Verdun (World War I) and Bastogne (World War II). Following each of the two stanzas that give a motorcycle tour of the infantry as a historical phenomenon, a couplet acts as a refrain: "O the ash and the oak and the willow

tree/ And green grows the grass on the infantry!" Apparently
wood from the ash, oak, and willow trees is used to make bows
and arrows, the first weapons employed by the infantry.

With modern warfare's mechanized ability to kill efficiently, it
leaves no honor or glamor:

> But at Verdun and at Bastogne
> There was a great recoil,
> The blood was bitter to the bone
> The trigger to the soul,
> And death was nothing if not dull,
> A hero was a fool.
>
> O the ash and the oak and the willow tree
> And that's an end of the infantry!

It is impossible not to read the *infantry* of the couplets as *infant
tree* because of the emphasis placed on the names of the trees,
the use of the word *root* in the first stanza, the historical treatment of the foot soldier from his infant origins, so to speak, and
because of the rhythms generated by the alternating tetrameter
and trimeter lines. Simpson is saying that war on foot was at best
infantile and that now, by means of mechanization, the *infant
tree* has been killed.

Only a closing line full of sympathy saves "The Heroes" from
the inclusive bitterness found in "The Ash and the Oak." In "The
Heroes," the speaker tells of dreaming of wounded war heroes returning by ship to the United States. The object of satire in this
poem is not the war which maimed the heroes but the way in
which the men have been treated by society upon their return.
The speaker dreamed of women's pressing close to look at and
to touch the heroes' "brave wounds and their hair streaked with
gray." He dreamed of the men's being greeted on the gangplanks
by cheerful girls with doughnuts and by a chaplain who "advised
them to watch and to pray." Then the speaker dreamed of the
heroes' being shipped to a "picturesque spot" where they were
given Bibles, medals, compasses, maps; and, finally, after the
catalog of small memorials, the speaker says that "They [society]
. . . committed the lot."

Until this point in the poem, the tone is one of the "almost gay
and comically ironic," as Stephen Dunning observes.[4] For exam-

ple, the wounded war heroes are called "rapscallions, those sea-sick battalions" in the second stanza. The metrical pattern of an iambic foot followed by three anapestic feet with an implied caesura after the first anapestic foot in each line produces a comic effect of sorts to supplement the speaker's choice of words. Until the last line of the third stanza, then, "The Heroes" seems an ironic but somewhat humorous account of the heroes' return.

Dunning argues that the verb *committed* is the fulcrum of the poem, which he calls "the point of balance, the place in a poem where a key word or image separates what has gone before from what will come." He continues that *committed* is deliberately ambiguous as Simpson uses it in this poem. It may be read on three levels: (1) in the military sense in which a "general commits troops to a particular action or battle zone"; (2) in the sense of being committed to mental institutions and veterans hospitals; (3) in the sense that "the poem hints that the 'rapscallions' lack personal commitment; they are pawns in a horrible game." [5]

Although the metrics remain unchanged, the last stanza retains little of the flip and comic of the first three. It is a soberly ironic account in which the speaker, particularly in the use of "fine dust" and in the moving last line, expresses his sadness at the plight of the wounded war heroes and his disgust at the gross way in which society has mismanaged them:

A fine dust has settled on all that scrap metal.
The heroes were packaged and sent home in parts
To pluck at a poppy and sew on a petal
And count the long night by the stroke of their hearts.

The soldiers appear to have been reduced to *things*—poppy-makers for their new parent institution, the American Legion. It seems reasonable to assume that Simpson, who returned from war a mentally scarred hero, wrote this poem out of personal bitterness. But he manages to keep himself distant from the personally bitter in the poem through the use of his speaker's dream as a starting point.

From the war poems included in *The Arrivistes* and in *Good News of Death and Other Poems*, certain consistent attitudes emerge. War is to Simpson, as Yohma Gray says, "a singularly ineffective behavior pattern if the human animal really wants to

improve his condition." Men in war, particularly those who serve
in the infantry, are led to combat like children in a schoolyard to
play a game with which they are unfamiliar. The men are, for the
most part, unable to understand for what or why they are fighting. War is a dehumanizing force; it reduces men, on occasion,
to what Thom Gunn calls "things, or passive animals." Yet men
in war strive to maintain their basic dignity as human beings, and
for this attempt they deserve sympathy. There is neither glory
nor glamor in modern war, yet there are heroes and heroic acts.
After war, the heroes, or their memories, are mistreated by a society that does not know what to do with them and that wants
to forget anything to do with war as quickly and as conveniently
as possible.

II *Love*

Like *The Arrivistes, Good News of Death and Other Poems*
contains a number of love poems and also poems exploring the
relationship of a man and a woman, though the latter are not
necessarily based on love. Noticeably absent from the three brief
love lyrics—"Song," "As Birds Are Fitted to the Boughs," and
"Love, That Wears the Moonlight Out"—are the humorously
clever and ironic qualities that mark the love lyrics of *The Arrivistes*. Each of these lyrics celebrates quietly and sincerely the
love the speaker and his lady share, but each in one way or another also brings in death.

The relationship of Duncan and Mona in the novel *Riverside
Drive* seems to provide the subject for "A Woman Too Well Remembered." Of course, the novel was published in 1962, thirteen
years after the publication of *The Arrivistes* and seven years after
the publication of *Good News of Death and Other Poems*. I am
not suggesting influences one way or the other; I am merely not-
ing that Duncan and Mona do seem to figure in this poem and in
others, such as "The Man Who Married Magdalene," by Louis
Simpson. Like Duncan, the speaker of "A Woman Too Well Remembered" realizes that there is more to the woman in question
than he is able to know. He asks himself, "Then is she simply
false, and falsely fair?" But he cannot say for certain. Yet the
speaker, like Duncan, is inexorably attracted to her despite, and
perhaps because of, her whimsically confused demeanor and her

blatant sensuality: "For when the stars move like a steady fire/ I think of her, and other faces fade."

The third of this four-stanza lyric reveals most effectively the sensuality and basic enigma of the woman that the speaker remembers too well:

> *Noli me tangere* was not her sign.
> Her pilgrim trembled with the softest awe.
> She was the only daughter of a line
> That sleeps in poetry and silences.
> She might have sat upon the Sphinx's paw.

Noli me tangere ("Touch me not") is a coup of ambiguity and certainly one of Simpson's most impressive images in the entire collection. Stated negatively, *Noli me tangere* is an invitation to the sensual; but it is also the title of a painting that reveals Christ to Mary Magdalene after the Resurrection.

Appropriately, "The Man Who Married Magdalene" follows "A Woman Too Well Remembered" in both *Good News of Death and Other Poems* and in *Selected Poems*. "The Man Who Married Magdalene" is in the form of a ballad, with six quatrains of alternating iambic tetrameter and trimeter lines and an *abab* rhyme pattern. The speaker is not involved in the situation, which is, as the title states, the relationship of Mary Magdalene, the sinner whom Jesus forgave because of her sincere repentance (Luke 7: 37–50), and the man she might have married.

The poem shares basic similarities with some of the Tilbury Town portraits of Edwin Arlington Robinson, a poet whom Simpson admires. Robinson often uses situations involving characters with severe personal faults or mental aberrations. One poem, "The Growth of 'Lorraine,' " deals explicitly with the relationship, which is not founded on the sensual, of a prostitute and a man who could not understand her. Robinson's major thematic considerations in his shorter poems involve understanding and subsequent compassion based on what is learned through the understanding on the part of both the characters in the poems and the reader. Often, the reader is led by Robinson to a state of understanding before the characters are even fully aware of the basic situations in which they are involved. Robinson rarely passes judgment on his characters, regardless of how cruel or misinformed they may be, for he realizes that total comprehension is frequently impossible to achieve.

In "The Man Who Married Magdalene," Simpson appears to be working within a typical Robinson context. The woman named Magdalene, who could, in fact, be any reformed prostitute who tried to live a normal life with a man who was suspicious and who was emotionally unable to forget her past transgressions, slowly wasted away, both in body and mind; and she finally died one night in her sleep. Before her death, which the speaker calls a "divorce," the life she led with the man was a kind of hell because of the quarrelling that continually arose from his suspicions of her infidelity.

Simpson does not pass judgment either on the real or imagined behavior of Magdalene or on her husband's obsessive suspicions, which, we can assume, contributed to Magdalene's death. The poet seeks, instead, understanding of the relationship between the two, a relationship based on love that, unfortunately, prevented the man from openly accepting Magdalene's new role as faithful wife. The concluding quatrain is both a poignant statement of loss and an ironic commentary on the previously silent acceptance of the husband:

> But when he woke and woke alone
> He wept and would deny
> The loose behavior of the bone
> And the immodest thigh.

Or, perhaps, the husband's pride is responsible for his expressed denials.

"Sleeping Beauty" is a companion poem to both "A Woman Too Well Remembered" and "The Man Who Married Magdalene," which it follows in the collection. The poem consists of three stanzas of eight lines each, with two syllables accented in each line. The approximate and irregular rhyming contributes to the staccato effect created by the two beat lines. The point of view is direct address to a man who lost a woman through death and who never knew whether or not she had been an honest woman. The speaker suggests that the "sleeping beauty" was a courtesan without actually saying so by implying that now she may be walking with Helen of Troy and Thaïs. Nevertheless, the speaker is not condemning her; rather, he is fascinated by her in the same way that Duncan is drawn to Mona. The kind of woman in these three poems obviously holds a great interest for Simpson, who embodies her fully in *Riverside Drive*.

III   America

Though Louis Simpson, even before he came to New York from Jamaica, admitted a great fascination for America, he does not use to any great extent material indigenous to the country in his first volume of poetry. In *Good News of Death and Other Poems,* however, the continent becomes the source for several poems; but these early efforts do not probe deeply into the shaping forces and into the current state of America as do the poems in subsequent volumes, especially in *At the End of the Open Road,* with the exception of "West," which is discussed later in this chapter. During the time he was writing most of the poems included in *Good News of Death and Other Poems,* Simpson was living and working in New York; and not until after he moved to California in 1959 do his poems embody America with originality and genuine excitement. It should be mentioned too that this move to California marked the beginning of a significant stylistic change in which the conventions give way to the freedom inherent in colloquial expression and in meterless lines—a freedom he finds necessary in order to express meanings beyond the surface of a subject. Nevertheless, the early poems on America are important, for they establish, or seek to do so, some of the basic attitudes that the poet later explores in greater depth. They show us, as well, the limitations that form demands when the subject matter is anathema to convention. Walt Whitman understood this problem and wrote about it in the Preface to the 1855 edition of *Leaves of Grass;* and he adjusted his form to suit the content of his poetry.

To begin with Simpson and his early America poems, I choose the opening poem of *Good News of Death and Other Poems* since its technical mastery is brilliant and since "The True Weather for Women" could not have been expressed nearly so effectively if the subject were treated in any but the most formal of ways. The poem is a satire on young, American, middle-class women who, for example, "in their April moodiness/ Complain of showers, for they cannot go/ Swimming, or to the courts to play tennis." The speaker then questions their concern about trivialities, which leads him to speculate on what indeed they might do if they are ever forced to come to terms with, among other things, "the full weight of the snow." The second stanza has the girls playing games, listening to the radio, and "killing time" in other mindless ways, "While thunders crack and summer lightnings glow." The mood of self-indulgence and selfishness gives way to serious exposition in the third stanza:

> There is one date that they will keep, although
> They have been often late to come to men,
> For death hits all such deer with his long bow
> And drags them by the neck into his den,
> And there eternally they may complain
> And tap and gesture in a frantic show
> And look at summer through a window-pane.

The parallel structure evident in the last four lines contributes by its rhythmic insistence to the speaker's seriousness. But there is a sharp reversal in the opening line of the fourth and final stanza: "Wind up the pulse with poppy, sleep them so!" For, after all, we are entertained by these women, and thoughts of death can really be no more than a small matter to them "When love is all their sun and all their rain." Thus the speaker concludes that they "will not know/ How punctual death is, or else how slow." The attitude at the end seems to have run the gamut from satire to concern to resignation and finally to pity for these girls who are unable to comprehend the forms death may take.

The true weather for women, then, is spring, both with and without rain. Structurally, the poem is held together by seasonal imagery—from spring, "all their sun and all their rain," to winter, "the full weight of the snow," which symbolizes the death they are incapable of knowing. One of the most interesting technical aspects of the poem is the rhyme pattern, which is complex and which, by its effective unobstrusiveness, works for the rhythms Simpson tries to achieve:

Stanza	1	2	3	4
	a	a	b	b
	b	b	c	d
	a	a	b	b
	b	b	c	d
	b	b	d	c
	a	a	b	b
	b	b	d	b

"Mississippi" is interesting primarily for the guise of Huck Finn as the speaker, or so he seems to be until about the fourth stanza. By the fifth stanza, the identity of the speaker has shifted from Huck to someone lamenting the lost way of life symbolized by the Mississippi River but kept alive in the works of Mark Twain, who makes an appearance in the fourth stanza as a riverboat pilot. But the poem, if examined as an attempt to define attitudes indigenous to the American past, simply does not succeed because, in part, Simpson is willing to rely on stock associations of the river and the Old South. Simpson tries to be colloquial in "Mississippi," but the sounds do not ring true, as they do in his later poems. The failure of "Mississippi" to convince is also attributable to its adherence to poetic conventions. Where conventions work well in "The True Weather for Women," they produce a less than satisfactory result in "Mississippi."

"Islanders," a 125-line poem in four parts, has the first three in heroic couplets and the fourth in couplets of irregular line lengths. The poem moves in a number of subject directions, from the origin and purpose of poetry to an analysis of what New York City means. "Islanders" is important, for it demonstrates some of Simpson's attitudes toward America and the American city, and it is one of the few poems in which he discusses the poet's particular relation to the world around him. Simpson himself is both the speaker and the "you" to whom the speaker addresses himself. Simpson is using the mask method similar to the device employed by T. S. Eliot in "The Love Song of J. Alfred Prufrock." In fact, "Islanders" seems to owe several other debts to Eliot's "Prufrock," from a conscious emulation of rhythm and image to a picture of hypocrisy and alienation in the city.

Each of the three stanzas of Part I treats aspects of discontent in the city. And each begins with a negative statement of the purpose and value of poetry: (1) "Poetry has no place, still you must choose/ A starting point"; (2) "Poetry has no place, but life is kind"; (3) "This tapeworm, poetry, won't make you fat." In addition, these lines serve to identify the addressee of the poem as a poet living in New York City who apparently is at a dead end of sorts in terms of just how he should work his art. The "starting point" for poetry hypothetically becomes "the displaced Jews/ Who come to this small park from the ends of earth." The speaker emphasizes the historical plight of the Jews, particularly in reference to the horrors of Belsen and Buchenwald; but he reverses his tone abruptly to remind the displaced poet of the poem that the Jews must be held accountable for the death of Christ. Here, then, is a possible subject for a poem: "Cry thief! Someone has stolen the true Cross!/ Go to these Jews, accuse them of your loss!," the speaker ironically exclaims.

The structural method of "Islanders" is association. One image leads to another as the speaker searches for meaning and purpose for his other self, the poet. This method is clearly at work in the second stanza in which the poet is upset by the speaker's ambivalence toward the Jews; so the latter tells the former to avenge himself physically on a girl, one who sulkily comes walking by. But, alas, "she's whisked away/ By a sport jacket and a new coupé." In the remaining eight lines of the stanza, the poet is forgotten, as the speaker, by the associative method, follows the girl with his camera eye. He sees her having an altercation with her parents because of her apparent promiscuity with the "sport jacket"; then he sees her packing her bags to leave for Hollywood where she may "hang over California like a star,/ Returning with affection fierce as spite/ To lavish wealth and set the old rooms right." Through irony ("like a star," "affection fierce as spite," "set the old rooms right"), Simpson is questioning the American spirit of restlessness, symbolized by the girl who will make it big in the movies and who will return to prove in the flesh to her parents that the dream can become reality in America.

Part II of "Islanders" is divided into two stanzas, each describing New York from a different perspective. First, the speaker talks of the city at night as appearing "sinister for miles" with its mammoth, darkened skyscrapers. He tells of his poet's being reminded of the Egyptian pyramids, which were built by "labors of the dead," just as, he imagines, the New York skyscrapers were.

Workmen in New York are exploited, just as they were in ancient Egypt. The subject of the second stanza is the automobile as a symbol for the American urge for speed. The speaker sees the poet "transfixed and caught/ In traffic—pale and spectral as a thought." Of course, traditionally, the poet has been out of his element in the city; he is seen here as typically confused and bewildered by the islanders hurrying in their cars, presumably to go only to death: "They're in a tearing hurry, to enrich/ The undertaker and to spoil a ditch."

In Part III the scene shifts to Times Square. The speaker sees his poet surrounded by marquees spelling out "Adventure, Passion, Crimes,/ Dances of Bali, Hitler's Loves, The Whip,/ And sometimes Shakespeare for your scholarship." These lines remind us of the earlier "Invitation to a Quiet Life" in which the movies on Times Square provide romantic escape. One of the major thematic considerations of "Islanders" and a summary statement of Simpson's attitude toward America at this point in his career finds clear expression in the second stanza of Part III:

> The blind man counts the nickels in his cup,
> But eyes go flying sideways, flying up
> Like dazzled birds. Beyond the daily wage
> They're caught in their own lives, the outer cage,
> A cry for exits, hoping to be shown
> A way by others, who have lost their own.

"And yet," the speaker continues, despite its impersonality, cruel exploitation, and hypocrisy, New York City has a romantic façade that is indeed capable of rousing dreams.

Part IV begins with an excited reverie stimulated by thoughts of the sea. As the speaker enthusiastically imagines his poet caught in the splendor of a romantic life at sea, he moves from heroic couplets to extended, irregular line length couplets, each line divided by a caesura. Simpson obviously felt that the heroic couplet could not sustain this emotional intensity. The speaker sees in the skyscrapers of New York the shape of an oceangoing vessel. This triggers his imagination, but the fancy is short-lived: "You find yourself at the Circle. This is no masted ship!/ Those towers are the stalagmites of stars that slowly drip." The new metaphor starts another reverie for the speaker; but, before he wanders too far, he cuts himself off: "Enough of these images—

they set the teeth on edge!" Then the speaker confesses to his poet: "Life, if you like, is a metaphor of death."

Despite this knowledge, the fact that the poet is a human being is, in itself, the important redeeming factor; he is the creator, the everything, and the nothing that everything is—to paraphrase from the poem, which, at this point, denies the three negative statements on poetry at the beginning of each of the stanzas in Part I. Through a "syllable. A word," the poem is able to create meanings. The starting point of poetry, then, is everything that relates to the human condition. The closing lines of "Islanders" reiterate the value of poetry as a vehicle for meanings, even though this ability, it seems, has long been forgotten: "After your death this poem occurred./ You were the honored fragments from the Greek./ After your death these stones would move and speak."

The poems "American Preludes" and "West" prefigure the direction Simpson's poetry is taking with consistency in his Pulitzer collection *At the End of the Open Road*. Both poems are experimental in technique in contrast to his early poems, which work regularly within the conventions, and both poems treat the subject of America. The lesser success is "American Preludes," which, after a narrative first section, lapses into obscurity for the remaining three sections. The method in these sections seems to be a Surrealistic interpretation of early American history. In recent years, Simpson has praised the efficacy of Surrealism as a poetic technique; and he has employed it with a large measure of success. But he has been careful not to use referents so personal that the poem only carries the weight of one man's imagistic associations. Thus it seems that "American Preludes," which does contain some impressive images and some firmly colloquial rhythms, is primarily a first effort by Simpson in what later becomes an accomplished method.

On the other hand, "West" is more than a rough experiment in colloquialism and in the use of images to carry the substance of the poem. It succeeds where "American Preludes" fails by juxtaposing the current American need for movement and progress with America's tradition of greatness embodied in the ancient California redwood trees. The setting for the poem in U.S. Route 101 in California where the speaker tells of having felt America's momentum in "traffic running like a beast,/ Roaring in space."

The scene of noise and confusion (Simpson frequently uses automobiles as unpleasant symbols of America) is balanced by Mount Tamalpais, a mountain overlooking the Pacific Ocean and San Francisco Bay, which the speaker calls the "red princess" that "slopes/ In honeyed burial from hair to feet." The serenity of the mountain suggests to him a life of "Ranching in Bolinas," which, he imagines, would provide complete peace.

Thoughts of the redwood trees start the speaker to imagining them as "whales of time" and "Masts of the long voyages of earth." Time, then, is the subject; and the poem's intent takes impressive form in the closing lines which, in rhythm, image, tone, and theme, are close to what Simpson is currently doing in his poetry, with the one exception of rhyme:

> On their red columns drowse
> The eagles battered at the Western gate;
> These trees have held the eagles in their state
> When Rome was still a rumor in the boughs.

The eagles stand symbolically for America and Americans. The Western gate is the Golden Gate Bridge, which stands as the limit of American expansion west. In addition, the gate suggests a westward entrance to California, the current American Garden of Eden. Physically, there is nowhere else for Americans to go; so the eagles are thwarted in the American rush for progress—the eagles, that is, as symbols, not as birds. The connection here is between the rushing traffic of the opening lines and the battering of the eagles, the latter signifying the end rather than the beginning. And both the redwoods and the eagles have been on this continent for a long time, even before Rome rose majestically. Simpson therefore is commenting ironically on the American rush for progress and greatness. He is reminding Americans that time indeed is infinite and that their headlong plunge is folly. It is interesting that the Golden Gate Bridge and the redwoods figure symbolically in the celebrated Whitman-American poems of Simpson's *At the End of the Open Road,* in which American progress and greatness are also objects of scrutiny.

IV *Classical*

The often talked about versatility in the range of Louis Simpson's subjects is well documented in *Good News of Death and*

Other Poems. There are poems on war, love, and America, plus three poems dealing with Classical subjects: "Ulysses and the Sirens," "Early in the Morning," and "Ægean." The first is a straightforward, narrative account of Ulysses' daring to listen to the sirens while insisting that the rest of his crew stop up their ears with wax. The poem tells of Ulysses, tied to the mast of his ship, listening to the sirens singing of Ithaca, of his war exploits, and of his love for Penelope. In this poem, unlike others based on the Classical or mythological, Simpson does not try to infuse a modern situation with qualities of a real or imagined past. "Ulysses and the Sirens" remains a good, rhymed, iambic pentameter treatment of a specific incident in the life of Ulysses.

"Ægean" is a lament for the lost grandeur of the age of Helen of Troy. All that remains are the natural qualities of landscape—bird and vegetation; the famous ships, temples, altars, and so on have vanished, leaving no traces. "Ægean" is slight but pleasant.

The best of the three Classical poems is "Early in the Morning," in which Antony answers Cleopatra's concerns of impending assault from Ceasar Augustus in this coup of understatement: "It's/ Too cold a morning/ To get out of bed." And—when Cleopatra, frantic for their safety, tells Antony they will flee on horses and then gather their forces later—he answers in this deadpan manner: "It's a cold morning." Then we meet the great Caesar Augustus, who after clearing out his phlegm, gives this order: " 'Corpses disgust us,/ Cover them.' "

The moral of this poem is that time is a force with which men continually fail to reckon. Time makes our efforts, often enacted in frenzy, seem foolish; it levels men and civilizations and, at the same time, holds great promise for us. In "Early in the Morning," Antony seems to recognize the futility of trying to resist time (fate) and death, its inexorable companion. The poem gains in strength when we remember that first Antony and then Cleopatra came to realize that a mortal life together was impossible for them, that whatever happiness they were to have was destined only in a life after death. This message may not be Simpson's intention, however, especially in light of the way he introduces us to Antony: "Spent with carousing/ With wine-soaked wits." Nonetheless, Antony's quiet acceptance does suggest a stoical indifference that was perhaps induced by Cleopatra, who was surely a goddess among mortals.

V A *Pastoral*

The summer 1952 issue of the *Hudson Review* carried Simpson's *Good News of Death* (a pastoral), and on March 8, 1953, it was staged by the Poet's Company in Chicago. The pastoral is not included in Simpson's *Selected Poems*, to the delight of some of his critics, like C. B. Cox, who calls the pastoral "not very successful." [6] Robert Bly, however, says it is the "most brilliant single thing" in the collection; he believes the subject to be the "death of pagan religion and the acceptance of Christ, and all that implies." [7] One of the reasons for conflicting critical response to the pastoral may well be its apparent tonal disparity. At times, Simpson seems to be deadly serious in his examination of the subject Bly finds; at other times, he allows wit to dominate, leading us to believe that the piece may have been written in jest.

Good News of Death is, I think, what Cox labels a "kind of mock pastoral." [8] The bucolic characters are there, as are elements of the supernatural; but the dialogue often contains turns of speech like "dementia praecox" from the mouth of a shepherd. There is, as well, a businessman in the cast of characters by the name of Cuddy whose early materialistic attitudes and whose later instant conversion to Christianity imply that Simpson is satirizing the modern businessman's devotion to the expedient and pragmatic.

In the plot of *Good News of Death*, Chloe, a shepherdess, is upset because she believes a life among sheep is degrading and not monetarily rewarding enough. In order to convince Chloe, his wife, of the long and honored tradition of the shepherdess, Peter relates events of the Trojan cycle; and he is careful to emphasize in his narrative that the glamorous Helen of Troy was, in fact, a shepherdess herself. Just at the moment when Chloe is almost persuaded by her husband to believe in the dignity of her calling, a sheep by the name of Roland begins to speak: "The secret's out. Your story breaks the spell./ My name is not Roland. My name is . . . well,/ Call me Orestes." Then Roland tells how he came to assume the form of a sheep. He and his sister Electra, bent on avenging their father's murder, killed Clytemnestra, their mother, and Aegisthus, her lover. The god Apollo—"(whose

strange ways/ I have not understood these many days)"—urged
Orestes to the acts he and Electra committed, which roused the
Furies up. To escape their anger, Roland had to assume many
disguises, finally adopting the form of a sheep. The Furies then
invade the pasture, announce the death of Apollo, kill Roland,
and leave Peter and Chloe dumfounded. The closing dialogue of
Scene Two contains this witty interchange after *Roland's* death:

> CHLOE: Oh, Peter, help me away, I can't stand more.
> PETER: This is more mutton that I bargained for.

The pastoral, or mock pastoral, draws to a close with Cuddy's
remarkable shift in attitude from the money-obsessed businessman—"I never stop for nobody unless there's money owing"—to
the devoted Christian who gives up his family and his business to
journey to the Christ child. So changed is Cuddy's behavior that
an unnamed shepherd is moved to say the convert is suffering
from "dementia praecox," and the modern terminology contributes to the mock quality of the pastoral.

Meanwhile, Roland returns to life and tells of the great powers
of Christ; but even his account of his experience after death is
not free from wit. When the Furies then return, crying they have
been betrayed, one of them questions the staying power of
Christianity but concludes that "the event will prove/ That truth
is always so." As Cox interprets the Fury's doubt, "Truth is the
fact of death, which men avoid by their 'dreams,' by their 'yearn-
ing outwards,' but acceptance of death releases a man to discover
his true self." [9]

Peter, who remains skeptical of the miracle of Christ, and
Chloe try to dissuade Roland from making the long journey to
seek the Christchild. But Roland, who will not wait the winter
out, leaves the shepherd and his wife with this moving passage:

> Now let the bottoms of the precipices
> Reëcho these immortal promises,
> And let the mountains tell through all their ranges
> That death itself is changed, that all things changes.
> And now we are off, there's a long way to go
> Over the mountains, in the cold snow.

To which Peter replies: "This is good news of death, if it is true."
What, then, does *Good News of Death* mean? The pastoral

does present, as Cox argues, a contrast of "Pagan and Christian attitudes toward death," [10] but what is Simpson's attitude? I think that Peter, if anyone, brings us the closest to what the poet believes. It would be nice indeed to believe that "death itself is changed," as Roland claims, but Peter and Simpson are not convinced. Cuddy's instant conversion to total belief is the object of some ridicule, but he is not presented, especially if we consider his closing statement, in a particularly foolish light, except, of course, in his appearance as a sheep. But even this somehow does not strike us as funny. Roland is a believer, but then he *has* returned from the dead and thus can speak with more authority certainly than Cuddy. Peter must be shown himself; and, while he does not predict the eventual downfall of Christianity, as the one Fury does, he is nevertheless unwilling to accept without reservation such "good news of death"—and neither is Simpson.

CHAPTER 4

A Dream of Governors

I *Technique*

WHEN Wesleyan University Press in 1959 issued *A Dream of Governors,* Louis Simpson's third volume of poetry, the collection once again demonstrated Simpson's expertise in constructing poems built upon, among other things, meter and rhyme. The familiar wit and irony are here, but there is evidence in *A Dream of Governors* that Simpson is on the verge of making a clean break from the restrictions required by close adherence to the conventions. For the most part, though, Simpson continues with the commitments he made in the 1940's—at least insofar as the poems look on the pages—to the neat stanza divisions, to the lines of regular length, and to the ubiquitous rhymes of the short poems.

Although reviewers were pleased with *A Dream of Governors* Anthony Hecht, among the most enthusiastic ones, recognized Simpson's artistry: "it is hard to realize how consistently excellent and various his work can be without reading carefully through his book again and again. This is one of the best new books of poetry in years. He commands a style capable of great emotional range, at once witty and dramatic, sometimes spare and ironic, sometimes frighteningly phantasmagoric, always inventive and not infrequently beautiful.[1] Donald Hall, who agreed with Hecht's view of the collection as one of "best new books of poetry in years," stated that "Louis Simpson . . . has written one of the most remarkable of recent American books. I don't believe anyone in recent times has achieved such a synthesis of wild imagination and formal decorum."[2]

Some reviewers, however, were quick to notice that Simpson's poems at times shone too brightly on the surface and lacked a certain commitment to depth. In other words, the poet's use of conventions seemed to preclude insight and revelation. This criticism was not a new one; it was voiced as well by some reviewers of his first two collections. Even Hecht notices Simpson's bright surfaces: "His worst fault, I think, is to succumb to a kind of lyric neatness, a too pat arrangement of lines and words." This fault, Hecht continues, is minor and "does not occur frequently." [3] Robert Bly, who wrote in 1958 that Simpson "should search for a form as fresh as his content," [4] reiterates his charge, citing particularly "The Runner," a long, iambic-pentameter narrative about the war: "The poet is describing new experiences and inner sensations, for which there is no extensive precedent in English poetry, with a rhyme and diction developed in another century for totally different moods and events." [5]

In a 1966 essay about poets published by Wesleyan University Press, Norman Friedman isolates certain qualities in *A Dream of Governors* that have bothered some of the poet's readers. Friedman's summary appraisals of the volume are especially valuable since they were written after he had examined *At the End of the Open Road* (1963), which reveals dramatic changes in Simpson's methods: "All in all, *A Dream of Governors* has wit, sophistication, perceptiveness, intelligence, variety and knowingness, but it comes perilously close to being a poetry of chic, avoiding at once the too-near of passion and the too-far of philosophy. The speaker of these poems is quizzical, good-natured, genial, charming, and satirical without bite, sexy without lust; he is never angry, or burning with desire, or impatient to understand, or anxious to interpret." [6] Friedman is also aware of the emphasis Simpson places on the efficacy of technique in *A Dream of Governors*: "It's as if the poet felt poems instead of emotions as he experienced life, and the transformation of experience into art took place almost before the emotion was felt." [7] What Friedman says is by no means the final word; but he has, insofar as certain poems are concerned, touched on verities.

"The Green Shepherd," the opening poem of the collection, represents, it seems to me, exactly what Friedman means in his criticisms.[8] In thirteen quatrains of rhymed iambic pentameter, Simpson, using for characters a shepherd and a shepherdess, examines the theme of *carpe diem* and the bucolic lovers' indifference to events that shaped the destiny of the world. In fact, they act indifferently to everyone and everything save themselves. I

do not want to suggest that "The Green Shepherd" is not a competent poem; it most certainly is. Humor, for example, is handled
well by imposing contemporary references on history—real or
imagined—in the fourth and fifth quatrains:

> A dragon like a car in a garage
> Is in the wood, his long tail sticking out.
> Here rides St. George, swinging his sword and targe,
> And sticks the grinning dragon in the snout.
>
> Puffing a smoke ring, like the cigarette
> Over Times Square, Sir Dragon snorts his last.
> St. George takes off his armor in a sweat.
> The Middle Ages have been safely passed.

But so much energy spent on stressing these characters' brand of
love seems misdirected, especially for Simpson, whose concerns
are rarely trivial. Of course, the shepherd and shepherdess stand
symbolically for lovers anytime and anywhere, but this knowledge does not seem mitigating. Neither does the irony implicit in
the treatment contribute much to our satisfaction. What is lacking
here is commitment, insight, perception, and seriousness. In terms
of technique, "The Green Shepherd," like many of the early
Simpson poems, is flawless; and there is a keen intelligence behind the poem, but not necessarily in it.

By way of striking contrast, "Orpheus in the Underworld,"
which uses the same meter and rhyme pattern as "The Green
Shepherd," is a brilliant accomplishment. After the opening quatrain in which the speaker laments "the long silence and unhap-
piness/ Of those who loved in vain for many years"—among
whom the speaker numbers himself—he tells for the next eight
quatrains of Orpheus' descent into the underworld to obtain the
release of Eurydice and of his subsequent failure to keep his
promise. In the following five quatrains, the speaker draws an
analogy between his own position and that of Orpheus: he loved
a woman with whom, for reasons not made known to the reader,
he had to flee "Through cities and the country of the dead." By
mistake, he "turned toward her," whereupon,

> With a cry she vanished.
> Goodbye, pale shadow of my happiness!
> I to the light have been forever banished
> That is the night, the night of my distress.

The closing quatrains of the poem return to Orpheus, whose legend, as C. B. Cox maintains, "becomes an archetypal experience, always waiting for the individual poet who must make his own way, to quote Lawrence, 'among the splendour of torches of darkness.'"[9] The images of birds, wind, and roses pick up the speaker's initial allusions to "nightingale," "the sadness of roses," and the "murmuring wind" in the tenth quatrain when he begins to dream the analogy:

> Then Orpheus pursued his lonely way
> Upward into the world, and a strange glory
> Shone from his face. The trees, when he would play,
> Were moved, and roses wept to hear his story.
>
> It's Orpheus in the wind. His music grieves
> The moon. He tells the water of his loss.
> And all the birds are silent, and the leaves
> Of summer in that music sigh and toss.

Friedman considers "Orpheus in the Underworld" to be a "moving poem about the loss of love, which shuttles effectively between Orpheus' loss and that of the speaker." But, he continues, "it is too artificial and mannered to convey fully the passion of the speaker's distress."[10] I feel that the formal structure—the meter, rhymes, and quatrains—of "Orpheus in the Underworld" contributes to, rather than detracts from, the emotional loss deeply felt by the speaker. In the first place, the subject is already charged with emotion—the loss of love; and the forms imposed by Simpson prevent sentiment from giving way to the sentimental. Also, the narrative of Orpheus' descent and loss moves rapidly and demands a sense of time which is best effected through the fairly strict requirements of the rhymed, iambic pentameter quatrain.

In another poem devoted to Orpheus in *A Dream of Governors*, "Orpheus in America," the speaker is Orpheus; he is addressing Eurydice. The supposition of the poem is that Orpheus and Eurydice have safely risen from the underworld and have come as early settlers to America. "Orpheus in America" is important for two reasons: (1) it represents a break from form and an experiment in a kind of free verse; (2) it pictures Amer-

ica (or the thought of America) as a continent holding great
promise. The poem begins exuberantly: "Here are your meadows,
Love, as wide as heaven,/ Green spirits, leaves/ And winds, your
ministers!" The regular meters and rhyming that we have come
to expect from Simpson are abandoned here, but the second
stanza introduces, in the rhyming of "shoals" and "souls" and in
the rhyme approximation of "leg" and "lute," the irregularity of
rhymes that marks this poem:

> Item: a ship, that on the outer shoals
> Lies broken. Item: thirty-seven souls,
> Or rather, thirty-seven kinds of fever,
> Item: three Indians, chained leg to leg.
> Item: my lute.

This itemization is characteristic of colonizers who faithfully recorded in logs or in diaries their experiences. I am uncertain
about the specific event, if any, to which Simpson is alluding; but
the point to be made is clear enough: early settlement was no
easy task, a fact which is reinforced in the third stanza:

> This is the New England—rocks and brush
> Where none may live but only tigers, parrots,
> And mute imagining—
> America, a desert with a name.

Tigers and parrots in this context suggest products of the imagination. This America held out imaginative promises to its pil-
grims; in reality, the Eden was rocks; the brush—a desert, like
the sand dunes on Cape Cod.

In the two closing stanzas to Part I, Orpheus is confused by
what he sees in the "pure space" of the presumably New England
coast. His Arcady "darkens like a lapse of memory"; he reads in
the glacial boulders "Columns that death has set/ At the entrance
to his kingdom."

Like the beginning of Part I, the first lines of Part II find Orpheus in the process of exclaiming:

> This gazing freedom is the basilisk.
> O for a mirror!
> The melancholy of the possible
> Unmeasures me.

The promise held by the New World is too much for him to experience, so he commands:

> Let music then begin. And let the air
> Be passing sweet,
> Music that scarcely wakes
> The serpent in her trance
> And leads the lion out into the dance.
> And let the trees be moved,
> And may the forest dance.

The closing stanza continues in an exalted tone to sing the praises of promise of this "greener Thrace," "this America, this other, happy place."

It is, of course, highly significant that Simpson works within a qualified free verse to treat the subject of America. The emotional responses of Orpheus to such an expansive land of freedom and expectation could not be contained by deliberate measures and formal stanzas. "Orpheus in America" stands, therefore, as an important precursor to *At the End of the Open Road*. However, the remaining America poems of *A Dream of Governors* bring us back by differing degrees to formalism, a later consideration of this chapter. One additional poem in this collection, "Côte d'Azur," experiments in free verse with measurable success.

Of all Simpson's poems to date, "Côte d'Azur" is his most conversational; it is, in fact, prosy. On the Riviera beach, the tourists—"The official from Lyons," "Dutchman and Swede," "An Actress in dark glasses," "heroes and heroines/ Of melodramas that are to be played"—are confronted by what Anthony Hecht calls a "particularly unpre-possessing petit-bourgeois French family," with their noisy children and all the paraphernalia that an ordinary family would take for a day's outing on the beach. The opening lines establish the colloquial diction and rhythms for the rest of the poem:

> Christian says, "You know, it's Paradise,"
> Mending his net.
> "The English," he says, "for example . . .
> They come and lie in the sun until they are
> As red as that roof.
> And then it's finished. They never recover."

After several passages describing the human scenes on the beach, the speaker concludes that people "cannot bear/ Too much reality./ Nor pleasure." "The trick," he continues,

> is to be busy
> Mending your net, like Christan [*sic*],
> Or active as the father is out there
> With all his tackle.

The father of the French family then nets an octopus. Children gather, and the rich tourists even become involved in the excitement, forgetting at least for the moment that they are indeed superior to the petit-bourgeois French family. Simpson's intention in "Côte d'Azur," according to Hecht, is to set this family on the beach "amid foreign tourists laved in wealth and fame and ambition and self-love, [and to] make of them in their vulgar simplicity the loveliest things in the scene." [11] But for more than this intent, "Côte d'Azur" holds interest for its experimental method.

II *War*

Forty-one of the seventy-five pages of *A Dream of Governors* are devoted to the subject of war, thirty-one of which make up "The Runner," Louis Simpson's longest poem. This subject, as Donald Hall once said, is such a consistent one that there is little doubt, as we have observed before, that Simpson is the major American poet of World War II. In fact, he is probably the major American war poet, a position won not because he has written considerably on the subject, but because of the qualities that distinguish his war poems, one of which is defined accurately by Cox: "As Simpson's imagination ranges over the history of the West, the many wars and the thousands killed, his characters appear to touch upon archetypal experiences which ordinarily we evade, but which are revealed by proximity to death. This hallucinatory quality provides one reason why he has written some of the best poems about World War II. Like Wilfred Owen, he presents the people and events of war not fixed by their particular backgrounds, but like shadows in some cosmic drama that involves all humanity." [12]

"Carentan O Carentan" and "Arm in Arm," two war poems from *The Arrivistes* which are balladlike and which suggest the childlike innocence of soldiers, seem to prepare us for "The Bird," a poem about Heinrich, a German private assigned to an extermination camp. "The Bird," which consists of twenty-eight quatrains, is divided into seven parts. Unlike "Carentan O Carentan" and "Arm in Arm," the first and third lines of each quatrain of "The Bird" employ feminine rhymes, causing each line to end with an extra, unaccented syllable. The second and fourth lines are in regular iambic trimeter. The effect generated by the metrics, the *abab* rhymes, and the quatrains is again a singsong rhythm, serving to emphasize what Simpson has stressed before: that the ordinary soldier is at the mercy of forces over which he has no control and does not fully understand; and the fact that the soldier in this case is German serves to universalize the effects of war.

The first of the seven divisions introduces Heinrich as a romantic youth who played the zither and who sang *"Ich wünscht', ich wäre ein Vöglein,"* so he could " 'fly/ Across the sea.' " Heinrich's youthful companion Hans, who wanted to be a soldier, went to war and wrote Heinrich at home that: " 'I hope this finds you fine./ The war could not be better,/ It's women, song and wine.' " Hans dies; and, in the second division, Heinrich has already been drafted and has been assigned to duty in a concentration camp, where, as the third division begins, his job at first is to sort the clothing of the Jews who were gassed.

Then Heinrich, who has sorted clothing so much that he has learned to hate Jews, volunteers for the actual extermination duties. As the poem progresses through the fourth division, Heinrich is depicted as still playing his zither; as wishing he were a bird; and, at the same time, as attending to his duties in the camp. But the Russians were coming, the colonel committed suicide, the SS officer in charge was found by Heinrich dressed as a woman, and "The prisoners were shaking/ Their barracks," crying out for revenge upon the "Bird" (Heinrich), as the fifth division ends. But the Bird, for whom the Russians searched, was nowhere to be found. Instead, as the Russian in charge of the liberation force was making out his report, he saw a bird "flitting . . . from tree to tree." The poem ends with a one-quatrain

division in which Heinrich, apparently alive after having fled
from the camp, is still singing:

> *"Ich wünscht', ich wäre ein Vöglein,"*
> Sings Heinrich, "I would fly
> Across the sea," so sadly
> It makes his children cry.

The suggested imaginative leap in the sixth division of Heinrich into the form of a bird prepares us for the imaginative liberties Simpson takes in his later poems. The symbol of the Bird
acts as the unifying device of this remarkable poem. For Heinrich, the Bird represents a symbolic escape from oppressive realities. As a youth, he had wanted to escape from the mine in which
he and Hans worked. In the concentration camp, he sang *"Ich
wünscht', ich wäre ein Vöglein"* and played his zither—an instru-
ment of escape itself—before he had to commit the Jews to death.
But the Bird serves an additional symbolic function: to the Jews,
it stands for Heinrich, the man responsible for their deaths. They
knew him as the man who played and sang before they were to
be executed in the morning. Thus an internal tension is created
through the dual meanings of the Bird.

By using a jaunty rhythm and by presenting Heinrich as a man
in whose fate hung many lives, Simpson is deliberately under-
stating what surely must be the most horrendous product of modern war. The subject itself is so emotionally explosive that its
handling could easily have fallen into outrage, but Simpson has
created a poem of great intensity which vibrates with an underlying horror that we, as readers, must ourselves imagine. At the
same time, we are made to feel sympathy for Heinrich because
his will was so totally destroyed that he has become a childlike
soldier who is unable to act as a man. The symbols of fallen authority—the colonel who has committed suicide and the SS major
who dresses as a woman—bring to mind "Carentan O Carentan"
in which the master sergeant, the captain, and the lieutenant are
unable to provide leadership for the ambushed infantry soldiers.

"Old Soldier" is a brief poem depicting by image and statement
a war veteran in a mental hospital who is awakened one night by
a "dream of battle on a windy night." A thunderstorm raging
outside imaginatively transports him back into combat. As it rains,

he remembers that he is in a hospital and "drifts into a youthful sleep/ Without a care." The poem ends with this understated irony: "His life is all he has,/ And that is given to the guards to keep."

"Old Soldier" is interesting for the colloquially insistent rhythms that the statement method allows despite, and perhaps because of, the commitment to a strict iambic pentameter. The poem is rhymed, but the rhyming in no way seems forced or inappropriate. Its unobtrusiveness actually contributes to the colloquial qualities, ones that work most impressively in the second of this three-stanza poem, in which the subject-verb, simple-sentence structure pounds firmly, creating at first a sensation of momentum accelerating, then of slowing down. We are led into the sense perceptions and corollary emotions of the veteran:

> The guns reverberate; a livid arc
> From sky to sky lightens the windowpanes
> And all his room. The clock ticks in the dark;
> A cool wind stirs the curtains, and it rains.

"Against the Age" is one of Simpson's bitterest poems about any subject. In four six-line stanzas of rhymed iambic pentameter, the speaker attacks the value of war, emphasizing the physical and particularly the mental anguish of its aftermath. Here, the subtleties of irony are abandoned in favor of accusation; image gives way to argument. It has been apparent from the early war poems in *The Arrivistes* that Simpson sees little to admire in war, but in that book and in *Good News of Death and Other Poems,* he has been careful to avoid emotional outbursts by relying on irony, by deliberately accentuated meters in the balladlike poems, and by the childlike aura he gives to his soldiers. But the first stanza of "Against the Age" contains the words *barbarian, liars,* and *murdered;* and, in the second stanza, the speaker places emphasis on the decay and destruction war leaves to a region, in this case Normandy. At this point, Simpson introduces the collective "we," who, it becomes clear in the third stanza, are the soldiers whose minds have been mutilated by war, the *"gueules cassées,"* which include the speaker.

What happens to these mental casualties of war after they return to America is the subject of the third stanza. "The Heroes," an earlier war poem, is an almost jocular treatment of the same subject, but there is nothing to soften the ugliness described in this excerpt from "Against the Age":

> Our minds are mutilated—*gueules cassées,*
> They walk the night with hood and mask and stick,
> The government won't let them out by day,
> Their ugliness threatens the Republic.
> Our minds are like those violated souls
> That pass in faceless, threatening patrols.

The fourth stanza depicts the singular way to survive for the speaker, the men for whom he speaks, and for all mankind. He argues that the only personal salvation and deliverance from this malignant world can be found in the mind, in "man's only state." But even the intellect becomes of small value, for "our lives/ Are lies of State, the slogans for today./ That wind is carrying the world away." The play on the word *state* underscores the total helplessness the speaker feels. The enigmatic clause "That wind is carrying the world away" alludes contextually to the opening line of the second stanza: "Those banners fade behind that blew before." The wind is made to stand for the destructive forces of war that, in effect, hold the power to blow the world away, apart, and up.

Thom Gunn, Robert Bly, and C. B. Cox all cite the hallucinatory qualities of the poems in *A Dream of Governors*.[13] One of the poems responsible for critical unanimity in the use of the term *hallucinatory* is "I Dreamed that in a City Dark as Paris," an unusual war poem for Simpson in that he is concerned more with war as a shaping force in the twentieth century than he is with war as exerting a specific influence on a particular individual, though he does use two soldiers to achieve his intention. His speaker is a soldier from World War II who dreamed that he "wandered" through the brain of a *poilu* (term used to refer to an experienced French soldier in World War I) in Paris during World War I. The setting of the dream is a deserted square in Paris during World War I, described impressively in these lines:

> The night was trembling with a violet
> Expectancy. At the far edge it moved
> And rumbled; on that flickering horizon
> The guns were pumping color in the sky.

"There was the Front," and the speaker continues that he was abandoned by the army and was lonely in the square. At this point, he realizes that his dress, rifle, and helmet belonged to a French soldier of World War I rather than to him. Above, two planes of World War I vintage—"The German *Taube* and the *Nieuport Scout*"—were engaged in a dogfight. The two concluding stanzas generalize from the particulars of the bizarre transformation:

> These wars have been so great, they are forgotten
> Like the Egyptian dynasts. My confrere
> In whose thick boots I stood, were you amazed
> To wander through my brain four decades later
> As I have wandered in a dream through yours?
>
> The violence of waking life disrupts
> The order of our death. Strange dreams occur,
> For dreams are licensed as they never were.

The metaphoric suggestions in the last three lines anticipate the imaginative leaps characterizing Simpson's new departures in *At the End of the Road*. War in the twentieth century has become a way of life, affecting death to the hyperbolic extent contained in the imaginative leap. The order, not only "of our death," but of our life as well, is disrupted. The closing line of the poem reiterates the controlling force of war on the mind of twentieth-century man.

The poem is committed basically to lines of iambic pentameter and contains some irregular rhyming. Each of the five stanzas is devoted to a different unit of thought, not to a specific number of lines, as the case has generally been with Simpson's previous poems. In addition, the lines move with a colloquial ease like a one-sided conversation. And, with the exception of an interlude of just over three lines near the end of the poem in which the speaker directly addresses the *poilu*, the poem is addressed to a general audience.

III *"The Runner"*

On December 2, 1957, while in Rome, Louis Simpson completed writing his longest poem "The Runner," a blank-verse narrative. The lengthy quotation that follows serves as Simpson's preface to the poem:

> This is the story of a soldier of the 101st. Airborne Division of the Army of the United States.
>
> *The Runner* is fiction; the episodes and characters are imaginary. But the fiction is based on the following history.
>
> On September 17, 1944, parachute and glider infantry of the First British Airborne Division, the American 82nd. and 101st. Airborne Divisions, and a Polish brigade, descended in eastern Holland, at Eindhoven, Grave, Nijmegen and Arnhem. Their object was to make a bridgehead across the Lower Rhine at Arnhem. The British Second Army would join them and advance from Arnhem into the plains of northern Germany.
>
> At Arnhem the British airborne troops were attacked by enemy units in overwhelming strength, and forced back across the river. The more fortunate Americans defended a corridor from Eindhoven to Nijmegen. The fighting, bitter at first, settled into a stalemate, and, with the coming of the rainy season, petered out entirely.
>
> In mid-November the 82nd. and 101st. were drawn back to Rheims, to re-equip and get the drizzle out of their bones.
>
> On December 17, they were alerted for combat. A German attack was developing in Belgium. The divisions were hurried by truck into the Ardennes, and on the night of December 19, the 101st. were digging in around Bastogne.

Although Simpson contends that "The Runner" consists of imaginary episodes and characters, he nevertheless records in his essay "The Making of a Soldier USA" the exact experience of being wounded yet still acting as a runner at the graveyard in Verghel that Dodd, the central character of "The Runner," goes through. Like Simpson, Dodd was a runner during the war; and there are similarities between the experiences of Duncan Bell in *Riverside Drive* and Dodd in "The Runner." Moreover, the graveyard ambush also provided, as we have seen, the subject for Simpson's early war poem, "Arm in Arm." Of course, the narrator of "The Runner" must be yet another mask Simpson assumes for the purpose of fiction; but there must be a thinline division somewhere between fact and fiction, though we by no means should read the character of the poet into the man Dodd. To do so would indicate on our part the most feeble instance of biographical criticism. It suffices to say that Simpson undoubtedly drew upon the facts of war as he knew them for the raw material of the poem; the rest belongs to his imagination.

"The Runner" is divided into twelve sections; the narrator is outside of the story he tells; and Dodd is the ordering device for each of the sections of the poem. Early in and throughout "The Runner," Simpson sets Dodd apart from the rest of the men in his platoon, not only because his job is that of a runner (one who takes messages back and forth), but also because Dodd has difficulty with the soldiers. Briefly, the plot goes like this: early in the narrative Dodd, though wounded, performs bravely and wins acceptance from his fellow soldiers. Later, however, the tables are reversed, so to speak, and by a series of turns, Dodd panics, loses his rifle, screams the password (thus letting the Germans in the area know what it is), and ends up dishonored in the eyes of the men of his platoon. So, the man who had already been decorated with a Bronze Star and a Purple Heart becomes the butt of jokes—the platoon's whipping boy. He is ordered to dig latrines, pick up the remains of cigarettes, and so forth. At any rate, by the end of the narrative Dodd is no longer mistreated by the other men and he seems slowly to be regaining their acceptance, to an extent at least.

In his shorter war poems, Simpson's attitudes toward war are revealed separately and in differing degrees. However, "The Runner" embodies most of the attitudes toward war and the military found in his shorter poems and essays. For example, Simpson's conviction that glory and honor in war are concepts of questionable validity is underscored in "The Runner" in the form of Dodd's accidental heroism. On being wounded in the graveyard, Dodd's first thought is relief: "I'm wounded! . . . with a rush of joy." The fact that Dodd is a runner (which provides Simpson a means for focusing in on him) seems only an accident as well. Unless otherwise ordered, he could have been just another infantryman, though he seems more intelligent and sensitive than others we encounter in the poem. Just as his heroism is accidental, so is his cowardice, the result of panic, which, under the same circumstances, could easily have happened to any member of the platoon.

The object lessons, then, of "The Runner," are centered upon depicting the chaos that war creates in the individual and in de-

lineating the circumstances that push men into positions of being
either accidental heroes or cowards. The effect of war on the
human being is one of depersonalization, for the active imagination of the runner was a cog in the machine that war would have
had him be.

The extended narrative poem in the mid-twentieth century is
not particularly welcomed by readers, whose tastes for stories
are satisfied regularly by fiction. Also, the narrative poem, if it is
to be received enthusiastically by readers who want more than
just a story, has generally to work within a new perceptual framework, such as a series of intensely suggestive images linked by
only the wisp of a story whose characters weave in and out as if
in a dream. Although "The Runner" contains instances of fine
descriptive and dramatic writing, it is nevertheless quite a conventional narrative. Thus it is not surprising that most reviewers
of *A Dream of Governors* and the *Selected Poems* in which the
long poem appeared find it unsatisfactory, by and large. Some,
like John Woods and James Tulip, are pleased with the poem;
but Philip Booth, August Derleth, Thom Gunn, and Robert Bly
simply do not like "The Runner." Booth argues that it "walks in
plodding pentameters and is a narrative (as well as wartime) disaster." [14] Bly, who has suggested more than once that Simpson
search for new forms, objects to the use of the standard iambic
pentameter line in the poem. He then asserts that the poem
"gives the impression of an experience of great depth, brought up
into very awkward poetry. The effect is of an unfinished work." [15]

I must disagree with the critical consensus; "The Runner" satisfies the basic requirements of the long narrative poem. The plot
moves well to its exciting climax. As the protagonist, Dodd is
well defined; we are led to feel with his emotional turmoil over
man's archetypal need to be strong, brave, and accepted. And we
can understand the forces working outside of and within him that
bring about his alleged act of cowardice. Dodd is no hero, and
herein lies a major point: there are no heroes, and there is no
glory in war. War is inimical to the human condition; and it is
especially alien to a man like Dodd who is sensitive and who
thinks. "The Runner" succeeds in what it sets out to do, and what
it sets out to do is significant.

IV *Love*

Both *The Arrivistes* and *Good News of Death and Other Poems*
devote a significant number of pages to love poems or to ones
that explore the relationship of a man and a woman. The fifth
section of *A Dream of Governors*, entitled "Love Poems," consists
of seven lyrics, of which three—"Rough Winds Do Shake [the
Darling Buds of May]," "Summer Storm," and "The Custom of
the World" (a reworking of "A Witty War")—appeared first in
The Arrivistes and have already been discussed in the second
chapter. Three new lyrics—"The Traveler," "The Lover's Ghost,"
and "Tom Pringle"—are brief, technically exact, and reasonably
successful. "The Goodnight," the remaining lyric from the love
poems section, is not properly a love poem, if by that we mean
only poems involving adult relationships. The subject of "The
Goodnight" concerns a father's fears for his growing daughter—
fears arising from thoughts of the number of potentially harmful
things that could happen to her. Although "The Flight to Cytherea" is not included in the love poems section, it concerns the
regenerative powers of love. The poem is conventional only insofar as it is metered, rhymed, and divided neatly into stanzas. It is
structured by a series of metaphors whose imaginative associations provide direction for the poem. The title is significant for
two reasons: The "Flight" suggests escape, an imaginative flight;
"Cytherea" in Greek mythology is the goddess of love and beauty.
Thus escape and love must in some way or another be subjects of
the poem, but the full meaning of the title does not become apparent until the closing lines of the poem. The opening lines,
however, establish the conditions prompting the "Flight" of the
title:

> There are designs in curtains that can kill,
> Insidious intentions in a chair;
> In conversation, silence, sitting still,
> The demon of decorum and despair.

Tension is created by the antipodal emotive and cognitive dictions in these lines. The charged *kill, Insidious, demon,* and *despair* work in a context opposite to the innocuous *curtains, chairs,*
and *conversation.* Into the latter three the speaker reads vicious

threats to himself, which certainly suggests that something is mentally wrong with him. In the second stanza, one brilliantly suggestive, the speaker clearly indicates that his current reactions to the state described in the first stanza—if, indeed, he suffers the same condition—are different from what they once were:

> Once, when I felt like that, I used to go
> Abroad. I've made my marches drunk on night,
> Hands in my pockets, pipe sparks flying so,
> A liner to the tropics of the light.

The nineteenth-century meaning of the word *abroad* refers to any excursion outside, such as a walk to a park or to town, and Simpson seems to be using it within this context. In addition, the word also suggests traveling overseas to other continents, which, as the poem progresses, is exactly what the speaker describes. When oppressed by his own anxieties, the speaker drank at night as his means of escape. The metaphor of the speaker as a "liner to the tropics of the light" is functionally ambiguous. But, read in conjunction with *Abroad, liner* carries the meaning of overseas travel. Also, the speaker made straight, as on a line, to bars, which metaphorically appeared to him as "tropics of the night." This union of suggestions is joined by another image of the speaker at night with his hands in his pockets and with sparks flying from his pipe that brings to mind the profile of an ocean liner.

The third stanza continues the night image; the subjects are people for whom the hours after dark serve as a theater: lovers, businessmen walking, and "the bum who calls you brother." The statement "Night is the people's theater" again introduces the escape motif. Already a contrast between dark-night (world of escape) and light-day (reality) is being established. The highly metaphoric fourth stanza heightens this contrast:

> And then, I've flown. I've risen like a sail,
> A plane—the roads beneath shone bright and bare—
> A black umbrella cracking in the gale
> Over an ocean blank as a nightmare.

Certainly, "the roads beneath" stand for reality, which, to the speaker, seem "bright and bare." And, in the third metaphor of the stanza, the speaker refers to himself as a "black umbrella."

Cracking, gale, blank, and *nightmare* describe the emotional state of the speaker when in the past he felt the need to escape from the reality he knew was himself.

By means of metaphor the next four stanzas reveal the places where the speaker's flight took him. He speaks of Paris, Africa, Monaco, the Alps, India, Mount Everest, and finally the moon. He may indeed have traveled to Paris and Monaco, for example, but the point he is making is that peace had no geographical name. In Paris he "settled down" "for a little while." Then, flying over Africa, he "floated on tobacco," which could mean that he smoked marijuana. In the second stanza, the word *liner,* apart from the referents already cited, could also be short for *mainliner* —the argot for someone who injects into his main vein a narcotic-like heroin. This reading, of course, is highly inferential; but drug-taking is certainly suggested in the tobacco image, and the descriptive ecstasies of stanzas five through eight could very well have been imagined under the influence of a drug. In any event, the "Flight" of the title reaches a dramatic climax in the eighth stanza when the speaker, after having flown over Mount Everest, rose even higher:

> And glided out beyond the atmosphere
> Toward the moon. It trembled like a bell.
> "Step right up gentlemen!" Then sudden fear
> Opened. I felt the precipice. I fell.

The moon often stands symbolically for insanity; the work *lunacy* testifies to this interpretation in that it once referred to a kind of insanity believed to have been caused by the changing phases of the moon.

The speaker's mental collapse was now complete and is described by metaphor in the ninth stanza. The down-flight of the umbrella is approximated by a rhythmic falling off in the movement of the stanza. The emotional fervor and imaginative intensities of the preceding stanzas are abandoned in favor of a sense of floating in the writing, achieved through liquid *l*'s and *r*'s, soft *o*'s, and *n* consonance:

> Down down like an umbrella I unfurled
> My bones. I must have fallen for a week;
> Then slowly and more slowly as the world
> Unwrinkled, valley, plain and mountain peak.

Oblivion through insanity is the subject of these lines; the speaker's mind was no longer able to function.

So far there has been nothing in "The Flight to Cytherea" to justify calling it a love poem, except for suggestions implied in the title. The love of and for a woman is the subject of the closing stanza, and it is the reason behind the perfect peace that the speaker describes. Light and vision, not dark and hallucination, dominate; and the stanza moves smoothly and evenly, mirroring the harmony now at work within the speaker's mind:

> And fell into the country of your eyes,
> Since when I have lived comfortably here;
> My thoughts are only clouds in summer skies,
> And everything is perfect, calm and clear.

The magnitude of the change in the speaker's mind becomes quickly apparent by placing the opening and closing stanzas side by side; tension and fear mark the first; serenity, the last. In the stanzas between, metaphors chart the speaker's emotional collapse. In this poem, the imagination is loosed; and the result is some remarkable writing. The colloquial quality of natural speech is also demonstrated in expressions like "Once, when I felt like that," "I've risen like a sail," and "I'm not talking of." But "The Flight to Cytherea" is, nevertheless, metered, rhymed, and divided into quantitatively even stanzas. In this case, Simpson's adherence to formalities works quite effectively; for the disparity between form, on the one hand, and content and expression, on the other, creates a tension of its own which complements the speaker's anxieties.

V *America*

Aside from including "Orpheus in America" (already discussed in Section I of this chapter), the "My America" section of *A Dream of Governors* contains six poems that aim at definitions of what the American condition is. With each additional volume of poetry, Louis Simpson is becoming more and more preoccupied with material indigenous to America; but the poems in *A Dream of Governors* reveal that Simpson as yet had not developed a consistent system of attitudes with which to infuse his poems with the meanings he feels belong uniquely to America. Interestingly, each of the poems, except "Orpheus in America," follows boundaries imposed externally, such as rhyme and meter, while at the same time the thought, language, and rhythms indicate new directions. Some of the poems in this section are exceptionally fine; others suffer by comparison. As a whole, the poems lack the totality of vision that serves, in part, to distinguish the America poems of *At the End of the Open Road*. This absence is nowhere better illustrated than in the prefatory poem to the "My America" section, entitled "To the Western World," which is certainly not a bad poem; technically, it is flawless, and some of the lines ring genuinely. But "To the Western World" seems faint in the presence of such excitingly perceptive poems as "In California," "Walt Whitman at Bear Mountain," "Pacific Ideas—a Letter to Walt Whitman," and "Lines Written near San Francisco," which are included in *At the End of the Open Road*.

"Hot Night on Water Street" is a step in the direction of Simpson as a poet intensely concerned with what America and being an American mean. He focuses sharply in this poem on scenes presumably from a small American town somewhere on a river and just across the West Virginia border. The speaker tells us, after the first line reiterates the title, that boys on the street were watching girls while a woman resembling a witch "Cried 'Praise the Lord!' She vanished on a bus/ With hissing air brakes, like an incubus."

In the second of this four-stanza poem, the speaker describes the street on which there was a movie theater "where I went/ To see a dream of horses called *The Star*." The turn of phrase "a dream of horses" is good, its lift away from the ordinary carried in the word *dream*. The idea of a movie suggests to the speaker the great dream-movie that America itself is: "Some day, when this uncertain continent/ Is marble, and men ask what was the good/ We lived by, dust may whisper 'Hollywood.'" The personification in the last line is impressive and represents Simpson's imagination expanding as it does in "The Flight to Cytherea." He has never, of course, lacked imagination; but each new volume exemplifies a heightening of his powers.

To this point in the poem, the speaker has been observing and interpreting; but he has refrained from infusing himself into the landscape. In the third stanza, he brings his own personality into play. By moonlight he walked on the bank of the river and, hear-

ing "An owlish train . . . huff and hoot," read dark, personal
thoughts into the train: "It seemed to know of something that had
died./ I didn't linger—sometimes when I travel/ I think I'm being
followed by the Devil." Whatever troubled him is never explained. We must conjecture this in our own minds, though a sense
of alienation (perhaps within himself, he felt disturbed—"moonlight" and lunacy) seems our most probable answer, particularly
in light of the word *stranger* used in the fourth and concluding
stanza:

> At the newsstand in the lobby, a cigar
> Was talkative: "Since I've been in this town
> I've seen one likely woman, and a car
> As she was crossing Main Street, knocked her down."
> I was a stranger here myself, I said,
> And bought the *New York Times*, and went to bed.

The combinative use of personification and qualified synec-
doche in the figure of the talkative cigar is interesting, but the
stanza as a whole is a disappointment. The flat, unimaginative
ending is in line with Simpson's intention; nevertheless, the intention here seems somewhat less than what we expect. The ending
of any short lyric is important, a condition Simpson recognizes in
most of his shorter efforts. With his America poems from 1960 on,
the poet is acutely cognizant of endings—as the poems cited in the
following chapter indicate.

If personal alienation seems plausible as the subject of "Hot
Night on Water Street," it is assuredly the major consideration of
the twelve-line poem "The Boarder." For Simpson, the alienation
one may feel in America is not a new subject; several poems in
The Arrivistes are based on alienation, but there the alienation is
city oriented. "Hot Night on Water Street" is set in a small town;
"The Boarder" is set in a town, the size of which is not known.
More explicitly, the setting is in the mind of "the pale stranger in
the furnished room" for whom the poem is titled. Structured simply, "The Boarder" is interestingly suggestive:

> The time is after dinner. Cigarettes
>   Glow on the lawn;
> Glasses begin to tinkle; TV sets
>   Have been turned on.

> The moon is brimming like a glass of beer
>> Above the town,
> And love keeps her appointments—"Harry's here!"
>> "I'll be right down."
>
> But the pale stranger in the furnished room
>> Lies on his back
> Looking at paper roses, how they bloom,
>> And ceilings crack.

Yohma Gray cites "The Boarder," along with two brief poems from *At the End of the Open Road,* as evidence of Simpson's ability to find a meaning that is common to everyone: "Even in the most mundane experience there is a vast area of unperceived reality and it is Louis Simpson's kind of poetry which brings it to our notice. It enables us to see things which are ordinarily all about us but which we do not ordinarily see; it adds a new dimension to our sensational perception, making us hear with our eyes and see with our ears." Miss Gray notices, as well, a related method at work in "The Boarder": "Simpson vivifies experience which is not a part of everyone's ordinary storehouse but which then becomes as real as . . . paper roses." [16]

In 1964, five years after the book appearance of "Landscape with Barns," Simpson indicated to the interviewer for *dust* magazine his new interest in rural America: "I think a lot of poetry in the last twenty years has been city poetry, but a lot of it is moving out away in people like myself." [17] The opening image excitingly weaves a personification and simile together: "The barns like scarlet lungs are breathing in/ Pneumonia"—an ominous beginning that calls attention to Simpson's dark preoccupation with America, a concern which more and more colors his attitudes toward the country. "Landscape with Barns" is structured by a series of contrasts: youth and old age, mortality and immortality, reality and illusion. The subject developed through this series of contrasts is the American headlong plunge into the dreams that the country cherishes about itself. The first stanza isolates particulars indigenous to the American way of life; industry, the automobile, and the farmhouse with, of course, a television set:

> The barns like scarlet lungs are breathing in
> Pneumonia. The North wind smells of iron.

It's winter on the farm. The Hupmobile
That broke its back is dying at the fence.
At night in a thin house we watch TV
While moonlight falls in silence, drop by drop.

The technique is to give one image after another in a distinctly
colloquial language. Simpson's imaginative powers are aptly demonstrated in the Hupmobile personified and in the synesthesia of
moonlight raining.

In the second stanza, the accidental founding of America is
generalized in this way: "The country that Columbus thought he
found/ Is called America." The speaker then states that America
"looks unreal" in both winter and summer—and especially so in the
summer "When movies spread their giants on the air." The word
looks suggests illusion rather than reality, a point the speaker later
reiterates. Then we meet boys who "drive to the next town, drunk
on nothing" to see a drive-in movie. Since the unreal in America—
its illusory quality—is so intoxicating, the boys have no need for
liquor. The word *nothing* carries the illusion which passes for
reality in America. The closing line of the stanza is weighed with
structural contrasts: "Youth has the secret. Only death looks real."
Again, the verb *looks* is significant; the suggestion here is that even
death to Americans is unreal; it only *looks* real, as, say, it is projected on the panoramic screen of an outdoor theater.

The last stanza begins with "We never die," which picks up the
attitude of immortality held by Americans. It is interesting that
the speaker introduces the collective point of view, thereby emphasizing the comprehensive acceptance of this attitude. He
continues:

When we are old we vanish
Into the basement where we have our hobbies.
Enough, when something breaks, that widows mourn
"He would have fixed it. He knew what to do."
And life is always borrowing and lending
Like a good neighbor. How can we refuse?

We cannot, of course; Americans perpetuate their own brand of
immortality, as is seen, for example, in the widows' collective response when faced with the problem of how to cope with empiri-
cal realities. The question at the end is rhetorical; for so inculcated

is this attitude that extrication is impossible and would involve denial of a way of life which began as illusory ("The country that Columbus thought he found") and which is daily re-enacted on television and in the movies. And, apparently, there is a comfort in the illusory ritual, which seems to provide the basis for American momentum. It is, in effect, responsible for the cyclical "borrowing and lending" characteristic of American life. Death is just another illusion. Thus the ominous beginning of the poem is tempered down to acceptance rooted in tradition, though the roots only *seem* to be there.

Simpson omitted from his *Selected Poems* the remaining poem in the "My America" section, one entitled "The Legend of Success, the Salesman's Story." I prefer to do the same in this discussion, for this poem seems more an exercise in technique than a fully realized experience. One poem remains, "Mediterranean," which Simpson placed in the "Old World" section instead of in the American group even though it concerns America as much as it does Europe. Like "Côte d'Azur," "Mediterranean" is set on the French Riviera and, in this case, across the bay from Cannes. The speaker is an American who is somewhat repelled by the Americanization of Europe, as it is symbolized by the movie festival at Cannes and by the television sets roaring "from the villas on the shore." He feels that Europe is in the process of adopting American "follies"; therefore, he prefers to "grow increasingly remote" and to leave.

Four of the poems concerned with America from *A Dream of Governors*—"Hot Night on Water Street," "The Boarder," "Landscape with Barns," and "Mediterranean"—cite either television or movies, or both, in symbolic or representational contexts to define the American condition. Thus far in his poems, however, Simpson has not found an ordering device inclusive enough to give him a framework on which to build a consistent set of attitudes. He finds this device in the figure of Walt Whitman and in the image projected by the state of California which we find in the poems from *At the End of the Open Road*.

CHAPTER 5

At the End of the Open Road

I *The Emotive Imagination*

IN THE Introduction to *Contemporary American Poetry*, an anthology in which Louis Simpson is represented, Donald Hall calls attention to a new direction in American poetry characterized by a "profound subjectivity" in the images, a colloquial diction, and an irrational imagination.[1] Hall cites the closing lines of Simpson's "Walt Whitman at Bear Mountain" to exemplify this imagination at work in such poems:

> The clouds are lifting from the high Sierras,
> The Bay mists clearing.
> And the angel in the gate, the flowering plum,
> Dances like Italy, imagining red.

In 1961 when Hall was writing the essay, the direction to which he was giving notice was in the process of being solidified, not by the conscious efforts of poets who wanted to pioneer a new movement, but by several poets—some of whom knew one another personally—who were taking imaginative liberties in their poems in new and refreshing ways. George Lensing and I call this movement the Emotive Imagination.[2] We feel that Simpson, along with William Stafford, James Wright, and Robert Bly, best represents the Emotive Imagination, though there are of course, other American poets whose work fits into this category.

Since World War II, two movements in American poetry have received the most critical and popular attention: the "Academic" and the "Beat," both outgrowths of an affluent society. The Emotive Imagination is indebted to neither; in fact, if anything, it is antagonistic to both. Academic poetry resulted, in part, from the pronouncements of New Criticism in which paradox, tension, all forms of irony, and multiple levels of ambiguity are highly esteemed as structural means and ends. Since the "Academic" poem is a structurally complex entity, it demands intricate analysis. The poem, then, is rational to the extent that emotion is not a major property. The meaning of the poem resides in its structure. The "Beat" Poem, on the other hand, is an emotionally explosive product, which, when compared to the "Academic" exercise, seems formless and which is antithetical in means and intent to the "Academic" poem.

The poems of the Emotive Imagination are perhaps closer in conception to those of Projective Verse, an extension of Imagism represented in the work of such poets as Louis Zukofsky, Charles Olson, Robert Creeley, and Robert Duncan. Despite the reliance that Projective Verse places on the efficacy of the image, on hard, colloquial language, and on form as an extension of content, its poems only bear little resemblance to the poems of the Emotive Imagination, primarily because the images of the former rely so heavily on personal referents; that is, the images often are meaningful only to the poet, not to the reader—which is not the case with poems of the Emotive Imagination. Although my intent is not to label Simpson or to put him squarely within the definitive boundaries of a movement, I believe that an awareness that other poets share similitudes of techniques, subject matter, and attitudes helps to place his poetry within a meaningful context that is all the more significant because Simpson is pioneering these efforts. Of course, he is an individual poet, especially in his vision of America; but his poems since 1959 do resemble those of others, and this resemblance is important to notice.

The poems of the Emotive Imagination are, for the most part, not directed by concerns for rhyme, meter, or specific stanza divisions. The diction and rhythms are colloquial; images juxtaposed to create fresh and invigorating perceptions abound in poems of this movement. Since most of the poems of the Emotive Imagination are short, exact timing in the placing of these images is an important consideration. The images in these generally nonviolent (but not always) poems create a muted shock effect insofar as the reader's expectations are concerned. For example, some of Simpson's shortest poems begin with seemingly dull and uninspired lines; then, as the poems progress, the imaginative leaps through images take place; and, in the closing lines, the reader is confronted with images that seem irrationally arrived at but that

contain the emotional messages of the poems. The reader is led to
understanding, therefore, through feeling rather than through a
logically charted progression of symbols. Assuredly, intellect is
involved in the progression and images in the poem of the Emotive Imagination, but understanding depends frequently on what
appears to be an irrationally oriented imagination. Coleridge's
"willing suspension of disbelief" is asked of the reader, who, if he
is willing to comply, is rewarded.

The imaginative leaps the reader is asked to accept are founded
on metaphors, and Simpson believes that metaphor in poetry
makes us "experience thought as sense-perception, and so understand it." Often the metaphoric qualities in the images that char-
acterize poems of the Emotive Imagination work through personifications. Stafford, Wright, and Bly employ the personification
method with more consistency than Simpson, but his use of it is
extremely effective, as in the following lines in *At the End of the
Open Road*: "But all night long my window/ sheds tears of light"
("There Is"); "And love is like the sighing of the sand" ("The
Silent Lover"); and "The light is telling/ terrible stories" ("The
Cradle Trap").

The poets of the Emotive Imagination also show a marked pref-
erence for subjects indigenous to the rural. Parallel with this concern is the attention paid by these poets to America, something
that few important American poets—excluding Walt Whitman,
Carl Sandburg, Vachel Lindsay, and Hart Crane—have done with
any degree of commitment and regularity. Since a later division of
this chapter discusses the America that Simpson projects in *At
the End of the Open Road*, it suffices to note that, although the
other poets of the Emotive Imagination work within the context
of defining America, Simpson alone has come directly to terms
with America's failure to fulfill promises it seemed once to hold.
Although this thematic consideration is apparent to an extent in
his earlier poems, this volume contains the substance of his vision.

If the poems in *A Dream of Governors* suggest that the poet's
style was on the verge of undergoing a major change, those in *At
the End of the Open Road* document his departure from an al-
legiance to externally imposed forms to the techniques of the
Emotive Imagination. Before the 1963 publication of the Pulitzer
Prize winning volume, Yohma Gray in her essay on Simpson's
poetry demonstrates an awareness of some of the techniques that

mark Simpson's new style; for Miss Gray had read in magazines some of the poems which were to be included in *At the End of the Open Road*: "He does indeed juxtapose images which are abstracted from their normal context, creating an apocalyptic quality, but the final effect is to clarify rather than to cloud. If his poems do not always follow an obviously logical progression, the total insight is rational and conscious and the associative progression makes ultimate sense." [3]

In the November 1, 1963, issue of the London *Times Literary Supplement* that carries a review of *Five American Poets* in which Simpson is represented by some poems also included in *At the End of the Open Road*, the reviewer, citing "Walt Whitman at Bear Mountain" and "In California," acknowledges Simpson's new techniques: "two of his recent poems evidence a new exploration of line and image which places him in the third stream of emergent American poetry today, poetry between the beat and academic, which inherits Pound and Williams but respects the possible renewal of more formal poetic shapes and searches for the deep image—a term which rightly belongs to the theory and practice of Jerome Rothenberg and Robert Kelly, and Robert Bly." This reviewer continues that Simpson does not, however, belong in the stylistic category of Projective Verse, a point well taken: "He does not employ the broken syntax and ideogrammatic layout of [Charles] Olson's followers or the short-measure intensities of [Robert Creeley]." Some reviewers of *At the End of the Open Road* show awareness of the extent to which the poet's style changed—as does Stephen Stepanchev, for example, in the New York *Herald Tribune* for August 2, 1964: "Louis Simpson . . . worked ably in traditional measures until about 1959; since then he has developed a brilliant new technique, reflecting the influence of projective verse and the deep image movement, which gives promise of new intensities, new reaches of feeling and consciousness."

What George Lensing and I call the Emotive Imagination, Stepanchev labels the "deep image movement," and Duane Locke names it "Phenomenalism": "Phenomenalism is one of the most exciting developments in American poetry since the ascendancy of the Williams-Olson-Zukofsky tradition and the vernacular experiments." Locke's essay on *At the End of the Open Road* contains some of the most perceptive commentary the book received:

"In *Open Road,* the style loosens, the lines become uneven, and the movement of the natural voice and phrasal breaks replace preconceived measurement. The imagery tends toward inwardness, and the result is a more phenomenal poetry, one in which the subjective imagination transforms by its own operations the objective into what constitutes genuine reality." [4]

It is appropriate here to examine several poems from *At the End of the Open Road* that exemplify Simpson's use of the Emotive Imagination and that do not fit into any of the categories into which this chapter is later divided. "The Cradle Trap" is brief and representative enough to serve well. One interesting departure for Simpson in this poem is beginning lines with the lower case when the word does not begin a sentence. This change suggests a general relaxing of convention on Simpson's part; however, not much can be made of this point, for Simpson is inconsistent in the matter of capitalizing, though none of the poems included in the three earlier collections use the lower case to begin lines.

More important, certainly, than the use of the lower case in "The Cradle Trap" is the situation of the poem itself: an infant in his cradle is surrounded by people, presumably his parents and perhaps other relatives, who demand that he return the love they hold for him. Although the speaker seems to be outside the situation described, he delivers the poem from the point of view of the infant. In the first stanza, the speaker lists by catalogue the external stimuli working on the infant:

> A bell and rattle,
> a smell of roses,
> a leather Bible,
> and angry voices . . .

The presence of the roses and the Bible perhaps suggests the day the child came home from the hospital or the day of his baptism.

The speaker isolates in the second stanza the demands of responsibility being forced on the infant:

> They say, I love you.
> They shout, You must!
> The light is telling
> terrible stories.

Duane Locke says that the last two lines represent Simpson's "new inwardness" in imagery.[5] The personification powerfully commuicates the effect of the voices on the infant and is itself a fine illustration of Simpson's use of one of the methods of Emotive Imagination.

The speaker begins the third and final stanza with another personification, in which his own voice seems to blend in with the whispered voice of the night:

> But night at the window
> whispers, Never mind.
> Be true, be true
> to your own strange kind.

At least the speaker is identifying with the attitude expressed by the night, the time at which the child is asleep and is thus freed from the "angry voices" demanding his love in return.

"The Cradle Trap," despite the rhyming of *mind* and *kind* in the last stanza, is quite different from the conventions of Simpson's poems up to those included in *At the End of the Open Road*. In place of exposition to establish situation, there is a spare catalogue in the first stanza. Instead of measured lines, the poem progresses by insistent but unregulated rhythms. The basic change is from observation and commentary to inward drama.

In "The Morning Light," another inward drama occurs, but this time it is in the mind of the speaker:

> In the morning light a line
> Stretches forever. There my unlived life
> Rises, and I resist,
> Clinging to the steps of the throne.
>
> Day lifts the darkness from the hills,
> A bright blade cuts the reeds,
> And my life, pitilessly demanding,
> Rises forever in the morning life.

The pains that the demands of the first stanza will exact of the "I" take rhythmic form in the first two lines of the second stanza, particularly in the second line. The speaker knows that what the day asks of him is, in fact, imposed by himself; and herein lies the tension working on him and within the poem. One part of him wants to live his "unlived life"; the other, to hold back and to retreat back into sleep; but his "life" is victor.

The closing stanza of the fifteen-line poem "Frogs" contains the imaginative leap characteristic of the Emotive Imagination and of the poems in *At the End of the Open Road*: "In the city I pine for the country;/ In the country I long for conversation—/ Our happy croaking." The four previous three-line stanzas establish the conditions leading to "Our happy croaking." The speaker begins by describing frogs that "hopped into the gutter" after a rainstorm, "With their skins of yellow and green,/ And just their eyes shining above the surface/ Of the warm solution of slime." Then he shifts to the night, with fireflies tracing "Light-lines between the trees and flowers/ Exhaling perfume," at which time: "The frogs speak to each other/ In rhythm. The sound is monstrous,/ But their voices are filled with satisfaction." The night products of the fireflies and flowers seem to be jarred out of harmony by the monstrous croaking of the frogs. However, the voices of the frogs are actually in a natural harmony with the tracings and perfume. Each product results naturally; the scene described is one of peace; the poem is probably about poetry itself.

Then the speaker introduces himself and draws an analogy, which is the substance of the leap between the natural and human conditions. He is, in effect, jealous of the voices of the frogs, which, as our senses have been conditioned to tell us, should sound monstrous. In order to communicate the joy that a conversation in the country can give to us, the speaker draws upon images from the natural world: fireflies tracing "Light-lines," "flowers/ Exhaling perfume," and the sounds of frogs croaking. It is certainly not uncommon, nor has it ever been, for a poet to employ the natural world as the means by which we are made to see the specific human ends he wants us to understand. Still, Simpson's method of perception is especially exciting in "Frogs," which, as Miss Gray says, exemplifies the poet's ability to make us "see things which are ordinarily all about us but which we do not ordinarily see." [6] "Frogs" stands not only as a fine example of the poet's use of the technique of Emotive Imagination, but also as a testament to Simpson's remark to the *dust* interviewer in 1964 that his poetry is moving out away from the city into the country.

One of the most curious poems from *At the End of the Open*

Road is the six-line "American Poetry," a poem searching after
definitions of both the nature and purpose of poetry in America
now. At the same time, "American Poetry" is prescriptive:

> Whatever it is, it must have
> A stomach that can digest
> Rubber, coal, uranium, moons, poems.
>
> Like the shark, it contains a shoe.
> It must swim for miles through the desert
> Uttering cries that are almost human.

These seemingly jumbled references point to the comprehensive
demands exacted on poetry by the heterogeneous quality of
America (first stanza) and to the difficult job poetry in America
has in gaining an appreciative public (second stanza). R. R.
Cuscaden has made some sensible observations about this poem:
"Today poetry must be able to digest the indigestible: 'rubber'
(jammed freeways, discarded tires in empty lots), 'coal' (world
dominated by business, industrial waste), 'moons' (new explorations which break down old myths and open new worlds), and
'poems' (an ironic comment on the reams and reams of bad poetry
being written today)." To Cuscaden's reading of *moons* should be
added two conventional symbolic meanings: love and madness,
both of which regularly provide subject matter for contemporary
American poets.

Cuscaden continues in his commentary to note that ". . . in this
same poem Simpson seems to be saying that the best contemporary poetry does have great, if perhaps destructive strength, and
that it flashes ('Like the shark') with an ominous beauty. Nevertheless, even as the 'shark' is confined to water, poetry's strength is
limited—its beauty constantly compromised—by the absurd: the
cast-off 'shoe' nestling in the shark's belly." This is perhaps the
case; but, just as the shark has "great, if perhaps destructive
strength," so also it is the crown scavenger of the sea, devouring
indiscriminately whatever it can; and the shark often trails after
oceangoing vessels in order to swallow the slops thrown over-
board. American poetry must be able, like the shark, to digest
anything.

The allusion to the *shoe* can perhaps be explained by the skin
of the sharks being converted into shoe leather, thus giving the

shark a practical value, which in America, with its pragmatic
materialism, seems requisite for the survival of poetry. The reading of the *shoe* as a means for the practical is reinforced by the
closing two lines of the poem, of which Cuscaden says: "For
Simpson today's poetry must do the impossible—'Swim for miles
through the desert'—and make a sound that is 'almost human.' In
other words, poetry must somehow reach and subsequently make
sense to a country which has little time and less patience for it." [7]

"American Poetry" is entirely metaphor, reminding us of the
great importance Simpson himself places on the value of metaphor, which, in turn, accounts for the impossibility of reading the
poem for any logically sound and literal meaning. But the suggested meanings are richly complex, and the poem remains a
valuable nonstatement.

II *Love*

Norman Friedman argues that the four love poems that begin
Part II of *At the End of the Open Road*—"Summer Morning,"
"The Silent Lover," "Birch," and "The Sea and the Forest"—"far
transcend in passion, sensuality, and significance [Simpson's]
earlier group of love poems." [8] By "earlier group of love poems,"
Friedman means those love poems included in *A Dream of Governors*, for his essay is concerned only with the two volumes issued
by the Wesleyan University Press. The love poems from *The Arrivistes* are witty, clever, humorous, dry, and ironic; and they at
times employ archaic language conventions. Some resemble Elizabethan songs; others, Cavalier love lyrics. The love poems from
Good News of Death and Other Poems retain the wit and allied
elements, but introduce a new consideration: the recurring figure
of a woman who is strikingly similar to Mona in Simpson's novel
Riverside Drive. "The Flight to Cytherea," with its metaphoric
structure, is quite unlike any of the love poems from the first two
collections and from *A Dream of Governors*, the volume in which
it appears. Despite the newness of "The Flight to Cytherea," the
poem still does not bear much resemblance to the four love poems
to which Friedman alludes. In them, subject matter, attitudes, and
techniques represent a new Simpson.

As in all but two poems from *At the End of the Open Road*,
the four love lyrics are neither rhymed nor metered. Their lan-

guage is primarily colloquial, which, in Simpson's employ, does not preclude lyrical effects. He has the remarkable ability of being able to infuse lines with the rhythmic motion exactly appropriate to his subject and attitude. A major difference, certainly, between the old and new love poems is the direction and degree of the poet's imagination. Each of the four lyrics ends with a metaphoric leap, which both clarifies and extends the meaning. In "Summer Morning" and in "The Sea and the Forest," the speakers themselves are the primary objects of the leaps; in "The Silent Lover" and "Birch," the speakers' perceptions are the objects.

In the first two of the four-stanza "Summer Morning," the speaker tells of spending a night with a girl in a hotel fifteen years earlier. The hotel was located in a "district of small factories" in New York "Where no one lives." From the window of their hotel room, they saw "Men and women working at their machines." The speaker's emotions are brought into play in the third stanza:

> Toys, hardware—whatever they made,
> It's been worn out.
> I'm fifteen years older myself—
> Bad years and good.

"Summer Morning" concludes:

> So I have spoiled my chances.
> For what? Sheer laziness,
> The thrill of an assignation,
> My life that I hold in secret.

Until the concluding stanza, the speaker's attitude seems to be one of indifference, a shrug-of-the-shoulder variety. In part, this indifference is the product of his casual form of address; in part, of the seemingly lax way he cites particulars. The first line and a half of the last stanza moves from indifference to hostility, as if the speaker feels defensive about not making something useful of his life. Of course, he is being held accountable only by and to himself.

A reviewer in the June 18, 1964, number of the London *Times Literary Supplement* calls "Summer Morning" a "closely felt poem about change bringing horror of illusory freedom," and the last two lines of the poem document the horror. The speaker, in an-

swering his own sardonic "For what?," comes to terms directly
with himself. In the fifteen-year interim of good and bad but un-
distinguished years, the speaker has become as ordinary as the
factories, the factory workers, and the toys and hardware. But
what exactly has he been missing? The title and the last two lines
provide the answer.

The title alludes to the particular morning he and the girl were
at the hotel in New York. Whatever else the experience they
shared may have been, it certainly was a personal and thus inti-
mate commitment between two human beings. The next to last
line of the poem contains the words *thrill* and *assignation,* which
to this point are the only instances of emotively charged diction.
"Sheer laziness" in the line immediately preceding must be dis-
counted, for the expression wears an ironic edge, but there is
nothing ironic about the closing two lines. The last line, "My life
that I hold in secret," is actually a lament for the speaker's inability to feel—for his inability now to become involved with any
degree of commitment with a woman. Thus he has been missing
love, though it appears that he does not come to this realization
himself until he begins to answer ironically the question he puts
to himself in the final stanza. Both the speaker and the reader
come to understanding simultaneously in "Summer Morning."

"The Sea and the Forest" is not so much a love poem *per se* as
a poem about the imaginative responses a French woman gen-
erates in some sailors when she appears on the deck of their ship
and from the speaker, whose identification is difficult to isolate.
An internal progression of point of view related to the images
gives this poem a structural unity that becomes fully apparent
only after the poem is allowed to unfold completely; and the
poem ends with these lines:

> All this, and more, the sailors
> Think of while she stands,
> One hand lightly resting on the rail.
>
> Farewell, my old pine forest!
> I might have lived there for a thousand years.

From the sixth line on in the poem, the various images of voices
rising, flowers, the house in Paris, the forest, and the "old pine
forest" of the speaker move from the mind of the woman on the

deck of the ship to the minds of the sailors and finally to the mind
of the speaker. Actually, from the sixth line on, the speaker is saying something like this: This is what I imagine the sailors think
the woman on deck is thinking about. And, when the speaker exclaims, "Farewell, my old pine forest!," he is saying, in effect: My
poem is going to end here. To the speaker, the "old pine forest"
has become a metaphor for the entire imaginative experience of
the poem itself. The last line, "I might have lived there for a thou-
sand years," is his way of saying that the world of the imagination
he has created by means of the poem is so pleasing that he could
figuratively remain there forever. But this poem, like all poems,
must end.

One way in which unity is achieved in this seemingly irrational progression of images is through the point of view that nar-
rows finally to the mind of the speaker, who introduces himself
into the poem only when he must close it. The governing images
of the sea and forest are as antithetical as possible as far as their
functional purposes in nature are concerned; therefore, their fusion
in the poem testifies to the speaker's belief in the great but transitory power of man's ability to create imaginative worlds by means
of poetry. In its imagistic structure, colloquial diction and rhythms,
and metaphoric leaps (especially at the end), "The Sea and the
Forest" certainly illustrates well Simpson's use of the Emotive
Imagination in his poetry since approximately 1959. "The Sea and
the Forest" is curious, exciting, and delightful.

The two remaining love poems, "Birch" and "The Silent Lover,"
differ in technique from "Summer Morning" and "The Sea and the
Forest" in that the endings of the former disclose metaphoric perceptions of their speakers rather than reveal specific states of their
speakers as is the case in both "Summer Morning" and "The Sea
and the Forest." If the quality of seriousness in a poem is a matter
of subject choice and attitude, then "Summer Morning" is more
serious than the other three love poems. However, "The Sea and
the Forest," "Birch," and "The Silent Lover" share this feature in
common: they are celebrations whose effectiveness relies heavily
on the use of exciting and fresh images.

Norman Friedman must have been thinking of "Birch" and "The
Silent Lover" when he wrote about the "sensuality" in Simpson's
love poems from *At the End of the Open Road.* The "breathing"

in "Birch" becomes "sighing" in "The Silent Lover," which is brief
enough to reproduce entirely:

> She sighs. What shall I say?
> For beauty seems to grow
> In silence, when the heart is faint and slow.
>
> Sing, sing . . . How shall I sing?
> In silent eyes, where clouds and islands gaze,
> The waves bring Eros in.
>
> I think the rustling of her clothes
> Is like the sea, and she
> A wild white bird.
>
> And love is like the sighing of the sand.

Depicting, respectively, the speaker's emotive responses to the
woman's clothes and person, the simile and metaphor of the third
stanza prepare the reader for the perception through the simile in
the last line. Despite the emotive quality of the poem, there is
nevertheless a discernible rational structure culminating in the
closing simile. Since in the woman's eyes "The waves bring Eros
in," the sand responds by "sighing," by rushing in and out as the
waves dictate. The perfect communication in silence, exemplified
by the woman's sigh and in the gaze of clouds and islands, is
analogous to the perfect harmony of the natural surroundings: the
sea, clouds, sea bird, and sand. Therefore, the speaker's metaphoric allusions in the third stanza and in the final simile epito-
mize the total harmony existing between the woman and him.
There is simply no need for words between them.

III *America*

When in 1959, Louis Simpson moved from New York City to
Berkeley, California, where he assumed duties as a member of the
English Department of the University of California, this move had
a significant influence on the direction his subject matter in poetry
was to take; for, along with stylistic innovations, came an intense
exploitation of America, especially the America of California. As
we have observed, Simpson's poetic interest in this country is not
new; for a few of the poems from *The Arrivistes*, notably "Invitation to a Quiet Life," more poems from *Good News of Death and*

Other Poems, and an entire section from *A Dream of Governors*
treat material indigenous to America; but only in isolated instances, such as "West" from *Good News of Death and Other
Poems,* and "The Boarder" and "Landscape with Barns" from *A
Dream of Governors,* does he succeed measurably in coming to
terms with what America and the American spirit mean. At the
same time, "Mississippi" from *Good News of Death and Other
Poems* and "To the Western World" from *A Dream of Governors*
contain examples of the faults that mar Simpson's earlier efforts at
working with America: reliance on stock associations and on surface perceptions. Curiously, "West," with its imagistic structure
and colloquial base, is strikingly similar, though it was published
nearly a decade before, to the America poems from *At the End of
the Open Road.*

Simpson's preoccupation with America has received considerable attention by reviewers of *At the End of the Open Road* and
Selected Poems, published in 1965, two years after the Pulitzer
collection. In my 1965 review of *At the End of the Open Road* I
indicated Simpson's concern with America in the tradition of Walt
Whitman:

> Whatever else he did, the inexorable Walt Whitman started the
> tradition in American poetry obsessed with defining what Amer-
> ica is. Whitman's job, though, was decidedly easier than that of
> those now compelled to define in verse the nation that has no-
> where to go. At least in the middle of the nineteenth century,
> there were frontiers—economic, social, and political, all of which
> were made possible by a physical frontier that still had some-
> where to go. Now, however, America has to turn on the inward
> spotlight to find a frontier; and introspection, especially when the
> past made or suggest many promises, inevitably lights up and
> focuses brightly on disappointments. A hundred years later with
> frontiers exhausted, Louis Simpson emerges with too much candle
> power to let the products of the American Story find any dark
> recesses in which to hide.[9]

Both Thom Gunn, the English poet and critic, and William
Stafford are aware of Simpson's commitment to America. To
Gunn, "There is also in this book [*At the End of the Open Road*]
an attempt—a development from a section of his last book—to define America, or the feeling of being in America, or the feeling of

writing poems in America." [10] Stafford, whose own poems are
built on the American land, recognizes Simpson's belief that the
foundations—the principles on which America was founded—are
perhaps more illusion than substance: "Again and again the
poems confront new, grim aspects of America's formative traditions. It is as if treasured documents like The Declaration of Independence should glow under a certain light and reveal odd
skeletons." [11]

In the San Francisco *Examiner Book Week* for December 5,
1965, Donald Hall, whose interest in Simpson's career as a poet
has been consistent, seems to touch directly on the poet's continuing and progressively complex treatment of America: "America was always there, bothering him, needing to be considered
from another angle, another kind of approach. At the start the
country was largely historic and geographic; increasingly, as
Simpson's imagination has become more daring and powerful, he
has dealt with the spirit. . . ." The London *Times Literary Supplement* reviewer echoes and expands upon Hall's analysis in a
June 9, 1966, review of the Oxford University Press edition of
Selected Poems:

> America is one of the poet's central subjects: the search for an
> American identity is the search for his poetic character. At first
> this produces the wide, idealized vistas of "American Preludes"
> [from *Good News of Death and Other Poems*] and "To the
> Western World" [from *A Dream of Governors*], placed above the
> landscape and the condition of being American; consequently
> the poetry has something of the generalized, orchestrated emo-
> tion of a national anthem. But as the poet finds himself, he touches
> down with more intimacy and confidence and begins a dialogue
> with the inhabitants that elicits the more personal emotion of love,
> anger and disillusion. The fulfillment is achieved in such poems
> as "Walt Whitman at Bear Mountain" [from *At the End of the
> Open Road*] and "After Midnight" [from *Selected Poems*].

Simpson has found in the state of California an ordering device,
notably absent from his earlier poems, for several of his America
poems. The figure of Walt Whitman appears as a second ordering device in these same poems, which include "In California,"
"Walt Whitman at Bear Mountain," "Pacific Ideas—a Letter to
Walt Whitman," and "Lines Written near San Francisco." Whit-

man's image of the open road ("Song of the Open Road" and
other poems) serves Simpson more than any other specific image
from Whitman. Although we could argue that Whitman's stylistic
abandon exerted a determining influence on Simpson's great
stylistic departure, I think perhaps too much could be made of
this possibility. Certainly, Simpson's apparent discovery of Whitman as subject matter coincides with his new manner of writing;
but other poets, including James Wright and Robert Bly, were
also writing and continue to write in a manner similar to Simpson's. Of course, all of them probably acknowledge Whitman as
the spiritual father of their poetry; but I prefer to think that
Simpson's style is more individual than derivative.

The influence, rather the force, of Whitman on Simpson lies
primarily in the subject choice and attitude—and, more exactly, in
providing Simpson with a way of looking at America, its spirit,
character, philosophy, and direction. Nonetheless, the attitudes
are entirely Simpson's; they are not extensions or refinements of
those Whitman seems to hold. Since, more than any other American poet, Whitman tries to embrace and embody all of America,
it is only reasonable that he provides a point of departure for
Simpson, a set of attitudes about the country from which Simpson
departs; for, assuredly, Simpson is not the optimistic celebrator
of America that Whitman is; moreover, the poetry of Simpson is
original in thought and in execution.

At the End of the Open Road begins with "In California," a
poem that establishes Simpson's attitude toward the dream America has held and holds about itself. The opening lines not only
set his tone, so to speak, but also document the poet's abandon-
ment of meter and rhyme in favor of the inner-directed method
of statement:

> Here I am, troubling the dream coast
> With my New York face,
> Bearing among the realtors
> And tennis-players my dark preoccupation.

In fact, the statement is so direct, so free from embellishment,
that the speaker is clearly Simpson himself, a new thorn in the
side of California. The "dark preoccupation" is a particularly apt
appraisal of the attitude projected in the poems of this volume.
Equally appropriate are the allusions to the California "dream

coast" (the embodiment of and the end to the American Dream)
and to the "tennis-players" who represent California's need, or
rather propensity, for outdoor recreation. Indeed, this stanza is
a most honest introduction of Simpson to readers of *At the End
of the Open Road.*

The second stanza suggests American history and literature, as
well as the American Dream, which is itself a significant ingre-
dient in both the country's history and literature:

> There once was an epical clatter—
> Voices and banjos, Tennessee, Ohio,
> Rising like incense in the sight of heaven.
> Today, there is an angel in the gate.

The "angel in the gate," which reappears in "Walt Whitman at
Bear Mountain," is explained later, since it appears in the same
context in that poem. It suffices here to say that "heaven" implies
a paradise in America, a Garden of Eden perhaps. The point to
be made here is that America did seem to be a paradise, or at
least to suggest a paradise, in its years of westward expansion.
In a literary context, the "epical clatter" could allude to the writings of Whitman as well as to songs indigenous to the American
pioneering spirit.

Walt Whitman and Mark Twain, the two nineteenth-century
American authors whose work most approaches a sense of the
American epic, are yoked in the opening lines of the third stanza
by the speaker's enjoining Whitman to "Lie back . . . on the fab-
ulous raft with the King and the Duke!" "For," as the poet continues bitterly, "the white row of the Marina/ Faces the Rock.
Turn round the wagons here." Both Whitman and Twain use the
journey motif: the former, in "Song of the Open Road" and other
poems; the latter, in Huck and Jim's odyssey on the Mississippi
River. And America itself is a journey, to which Simpson bears
witness in the title of this collection of poems; but the journey ends
at the Pacific Ocean, a figure Simpson employs again and quite appropriately in "Lines Written near San Francisco," the last poem
of the volume. The "wagons" in the last line of the third stanza
allude to the wagon trains that brought settlers to the West; and,
with the settling of California, the frontier, in effect, ceased to
be. What remains fronting San Francisco Bay is Alcatraz, "the

Rock." The speaker, then, is providing a second answer, in addition to the Pacific Ocean, to the question of what is at the end of the open road: a prison.

Whitman is enjoined to "Lie back!" a second time in the opening line of the fourth stanza. The speaker then shifts point of view from "I" and the implied "you" to the collective "we," to emphasize that the conditions of which he talks have meaning to all Americans:

> Lie back! We cannot bear
> The stars any more, those infinite spaces.
> Let the realtors divide the mountain,
> For they have already subdivided the valley.

The speaker's irony is aimed not only at the realtors but also at the American penchant for moving forward—for progressing toward anything anywhere. However, since we cannot do anything about the "stars" (space exploration had not yet been a major American effort) and since "those infinite spaces" bother us by the fact of just *being* there, we must find somewhere to continue our pioneering efforts. So we cut into the mountain, after having already civilized the valley. But, again, where are we really going? What are we really accomplishing? These answers follow in a remarkably ironic stanza:

> Rectangular city blocks astonished
> Herodotus in Babylon,
> Cortez in Tenochtitlan,
> And here's the same old city-planner, death.

Just as Herodotus, "The Father of History," and Hernando de Cortez, the Spanish conquistador, must have been astonished when they saw the architecture of Babylon, the capital of Babylonia, and Tenochtitlan, the capital of the Aztec Empire, so must we be astonished when we realize that our own empire ends with the "rectangular city blocks" of Alcatraz. Great empires perish; the "same old city-planner, death," is working on the American empire as it did to the Mesopotamian and Aztec empires. The figure of "death" will appear later in subsequent poems by Simpson.

Despite this knowledge of forthcoming demise, the American Dream continues to prevail, as "In California" concludes:

> We cannot turn or stay.
> For though we sleep, and let the reins fall slack,
> The great cloud-wagons move
> Outward still, dreaming of a Pacific.

We are still unable to conceive and thus accept that our boundaries, physical and perhaps also spiritual, have already been defined. Bodily "we sleep, and let the reins fall slack" on the animals drawing our prairie-schooners westward. Yet we are so inexorably committed to motion that we are unable to draw the reins back on our spirit; therefore, we dream of "a Pacific" out there somewhere, toward which the wagons of our mind move.

"Walt Whitman at Bear Mountain" is Simpson's most important and best poem; it ranks, in fact, as one of the most significant lyrics in the canon of American poetry. The title and description of the first five lines refer to the statue of Walt Whitman at Bear Mountain State Park in New York State. The allusion in the third line to "death and lilacs" refers to "When Lilacs Last in Dooryard Bloom'd," the poem in which Whitman's most consistently impressive writing is found. The description of Whitman in these lines is engaging and demonstrates Simpson's fondness for Whitman's poetry. But "Walt Whitman at Bear Mountain" is more than an engaging celebration; it is a serious indictment of the American condition and, at the same time, an exoneration of Whitman from the frequent charge that his poetry prophesies the fulfillment of the promises America held in the nineteenth century.

Certainly, a key to one thematic consideration in this poem is spoken clearly by the "poet of death and lilacs" himself, in the guise of his statue: "Yet, did I not warn you that it was Myself/ I advertised? Were my words not sufficiently plain?" The image of the used-car lot—"The Open Road goes to the used-car lot"—is especially telling, for the automobile in America has come to mean much more than just a means of transportation: it is a status symbol, a way of life, and the American need for motion. The reference to the houses and snow in lines 11–12 is ironic, the implication being that snow (outer weather) is the only weight the

houses (and their occupants) can sustain. The image of the light
in line 13 is picked up later in the poem in reference to the contracting of "American dreams" as a disease.

Whitman's personified statue is quick to respond and to repri-
mand the speaker for assuming that his own moods are the bases
for prophecy: "Yet, did I not warn you that it was Myself/ I advertised? Were my words not sufficiently plain?" Despite the admiration Simpson obviously holds for Whitman, he is perfectly
aware that Whitman is an egoist who advertises himself in his
poetry; and this recognition accounts for the statue's delight in
being found out. There is also a suggestion here—a functional
ambiguity of sorts—that Whitman would indeed derive pleasure
in having deceived his critical public into believing in his role as
prophet. In any event, the speaker concludes Whitman's active
presence in the poem with a particularly good image of the poet:
"A crocodile in wrinkled metal loafing." There is an allusion to
Whitman's statue loafing in the fourth line of the poem; in his
own poetry, Whitman at times does refer to himself as a loafer.

Simpson's indictment of the American condition is the dominant theme of the second part—from line 27 to the end of the
poem—of "Walt Whitman at Bear Mountain." "American dreams"
in line 31 emerges as a deafness, the inability to hear properly,
which, I am assuming, is related to listening symbolically to the
wrong sounds in the poetry of Walt Whitman. The analogy, however, goes further: the speaker learns that he had been misin-
terpreting the poetry of Whitman. With this knowledge as a
starting point, the speaker states that, just as Whitman has been
listened to wrongly, so too has America been listening wrongly
to itself. Perhaps the promises that seemed so much an inherent
quality of the nature of America were really nonexistent. Perhaps
the American people have been misled by this mirage of promises
into thinking their country is a Garden of Eden. Only the country
store owner, the "dumb" housewife, and the earth have not been
stricken by the disease of "American dreams"; for they have been
conditioned to humility and thus do not expect to create microcosmic empires.

Aware of the inherent wrongness underscoring the American
Dream, the speaker is forced into exclaiming: "All that grave
weight of America/ Cancelled!" The pun on the word *grave*
seems intentional. What then remains for America? What can we

do with ourselves and our country now that the truth is finally known? The closing lines of the next to the last stanza dramatize metaphorically his answers: everything is coming down ("Unbuilding") since there was nothing ("stones that are not there") to build on in the first place—to build, that is, as we *have built*. The word *castles* in this stanza probably means materialistic castles—factories, business establishments, and the like. The American expression "A man's home is his castle" would not, I think, be applicable here as an equivalent for "These houses built of wood. . . ." *Roses* probably stands for the false hope and promises that were always "Blossoming. . . ."

The last four lines of "Walt Whitman at Bear Mountain," which are reproduced in the opening paragraph of this chapter, have frequently been cited by Simpson's critics and reviewers as a brilliantly imagistic ending to an outstanding poem. But no one has yet offered an explanation for the rational sense of these lines. The fact that they are striking and, at the same time, seemingly inexplicable is strong testimony to the efficacy of the Emotive Imagination. The images work on the reader independently of their rational content. He feels that something is being illuminated, but he is uncertain as to exactly what. Put to the test of explication, the reader may offer this: The physical setting crosses the continent from Bear Mountain State Park in New York to San Francisco Bay and the Golden Gate Bridge. The air is clearing; thus the "angel in the gate" (perhaps the figure of one carved on the Bridge) is pleased and dances, imagining some excitement in the offing or already taking place. Put to the symbolic test, the reader may offer this: Now that we (Americans) understand the reasons for our disease ("American dreams"), we can rejoice and begin "living" again. The "angel in the gate" becomes the angel in the Garden of Eden; California is our Eden. In any event, these readings were in my mind when I wrote to Simpson, asking in particular about the "angel in the gate," which appears also in "In California." His reply, dated August 3, 1967, contains the following explanation:

No, there's no figure of an angel on the Golden Gate bridge. The image at the end of Walt Whitman ["Walt Whitman at Bear Mountain"] is a composite of: (1) The angel of Eden, (2) a plum tree, magenta-colored, that I had at the time.

Maybe (1) needs more explanation. The point of the argument is that Americans might try not being so expansive, for a change; not being programmed for empire. If they waited, then, as Rilke suggests in the Duino elegies, "happiness" might fall. A Renaissance is graceful. Then the "angel in the gate"—here symbolized as a plum-tree, a color that is given, not created by an act of will—would rejoice. My angel is the dance of "the given" (though, as I've suggested above, it was suggested also by the old angel of Eden, driving man out to a life of will. Here, if you like, the angel's job is over.).

I can think of no other recent poem about America which so incisively and artistically probes at the core of the American spirit. Even in a literary sense, Simpson has provided a valuable service by placing Whitman's so-called prophecies in a sensible and meaningful perspective. In addition and more importantly, Simpson has questioned the validity of "American dreams." Our headlong plunge into self-aggrandizement is the primary object of his indictment. His prescription is offered in the perhaps too confusing closing lines of the poem.

Stylistically, "Walt Whitman at Bear Mountain" is as equally impressive as it is in terms of thematic significance. The personified statue of Walt Whitman acts as genesis and ordering device for the first twenty-six lines. Then the larger concerns of the American condition, concerns developing naturally from the first part of the poem, occupy the remaining lines. Diction and rhythm are distinctly conversational, which, of course, is only proper since the poem is, in part, a dialogue. Simpson's use of enjambment to assist in conveying the quality of natural speech is especially effective here: "These houses built of wood sustain/ Colossal snows." The syllabic heaviness of the word *Colossal* carries with it the weight of the snow. The image of the statue in the opening lines, the crocodile figure, and the images in the last two lines of the poem are exceptionally good. If it has not already become so (and there is reason to believe it has), "Walt Whitman at Bear Mountain" is destined to become an "event poem"—a poem not only excellent in itself but an authoritative one as well.

"Pacific Ideas—a Letter to Walt Whitman" again indicts an aspect of the American condition; then it curiously turns inward and concludes by focusing not too clearly on the speaker himself.

The opening stanza calls to mind, as in "In California," the wagon trains moving westward; then images are effectively juxtaposed:

> When the schooners were drifting
> Over the hills—schooners like white skulls—
> The sun was the clock in that parlor
> And the piano was played by the wind.

The second stanza begins with the word *But*, a word in modern poetry usually indicating that a sharp reversal or shock of some sort is to follow. In this case, it is suggested, but not explicitly stated, that the American spirit to move must eventually stop. The speaker continues that "things" (material possessions) "are necessary," after which Walt Whitman is addressed: "Those 'immensely overpaid accounts,'/ Walt, it seems that we must pay them again." The quotation the speaker cites comes from Whitman's "Song of the Exposition" in the following context:

> Come Muse migrate from Greece and Ionia,
> Cross out please those immensely overpaid accounts.
> That matter of Troy, and Achilles' wrath, and AEneas',
>   Odysseus' wanderings.
> Placard "Removed" and "To Let" on the rocks of your
>   snowy Parnassus. . . .
>
> For know a better, fresher, busier sphere, a wide,
>   untried domain awaits, demands you.

Whitman is invoking the Muse to make both himself as a poet and America as a country forget the Old World as far as, among other considerations, subject matter for poetry is concerned. The "immensely overpaid accounts" are debts paid over and over again to heritage and history, both real and imagined, that are exerting influences overwhelmingly out of proportion. Whitman wants new subjects for a New World.

Although Whitman's "immensely overpaid accounts" (at least in the context in which it appears above) relate primarily to the writing of poetry, this use is not the one to which Simpson puts the phrase in "Pacific Ideas—a Letter to Walt Whitman." Rather, Simpson is concerned with the way in which America is being civilized as a nation and society. In the third stanza, the speaker

tells of the difficulties inherent in solidifying a society destined
for greatness:

> It's hard to civilize, to change
> The usual order;
> And the young, who are always the same, endlessly
> Rehearse the fate of Achilles.

It is hard, he means, to alter the pattern by which a society grows
into greatness. The young leaders of a young, emerging country
have the identical ends in mind as the young leaders had of earlier civilizations; they are guilty of pride, "the fate of Achilles."
It is interesting to note that Simpson cites Achilles just as Whitman does in "Song of the Exposition," but there is a contextual
difference. The poem closes with these lyrical and strange lines:

> But here is the sea and the mist,
> Gray Lethe of forgetfulness,
> And the moon, gliding from the mist,
> Love, with her garland of dreams.
>
> And I have quarrelled with my books
> For the moon is not in their fable,
> And say to the darkness, Let your dragon come,
> O anything, to hold her in my arms!

The change in language and rhythm from the first four stanzas to
the last two is one from colloquial statement to lyrical intensity.
The new direction is from the external of Walt Whitman, America, business executives of the "upper floors," and English profes-
sors to the internal of the speaker's emotions. Facing the Pacific
Ocean, the westward limit to physical expansion, the speaker is
caught in the romantic mood created by mist over the ocean. That
he has "quarrelled" with his books serves to link him with Whitman, a professed antiacademician. The exotic setting exerts a
Lethelike influence over the speaker; he forgets the concerns that
prompted the "Letter" to Whitman in the first place, and he
seems to emerge with a plea for Love, personified as the moon
"gliding from the mist," to come to him regardless of what perils
she may bring. I am reminded here of Whitman's short lyric
"When I Heard the Learn'd Astronomer," in which the poet has

had enough of an astronomer's discourse on the scientific prop-
erties of stars, and so goes out into the night: "Till rising and
gliding out I wander'd off by myself,/ Into the mystical moist
night-air, and from time to time,/ Look'd up in perfect silence at
the stars." Something of the same seems to have happened to
Simpson's speaker, who, like Whitman's, uses the word *gliding*
and feels a touch of wetness in the night air.

Appropriately, the final poem of *At the End of the Open Road*
and the final one in which Walt Whitman figures significantly is
"Lines Written near San Francisco." Consisting of three nine-
stanza parts, each stanza having three lines, it is one of the longer
poems of the collection. Despite the stanza consistency, there is
neither rhyming nor a metrical pattern; both diction and rhythms
are based in the colloquial. Whitman does not appear in the poem
until the final section and then only in terms of a single reference,
but the reference is important. "Lines Written near San Francisco" assimilates Simpson's attitudes toward America found in
the three previous California-Whitman poems and in the remaining America poems to be considered shortly.

The poem opens with a dramatization of the San Francisco
earthquake and fire of 1906. The central figure is the great op-
eratic tenor Enrico Caruso, who is presented as having been in
the act of performing when the tremors began. Then characters
from operas—Otello, Don Giovanni, Figaro, and Lucia—imaginatively act out their roles during the live performance of the natural disaster. Part I concludes with Death, the central character
of the poem, seen at rest after the "tremors/ Passed under the
waves."

Part II is involved with the efforts to rebuild San Francisco.
A "bowler-hatted" engineer is writing down (there is a shift to
present tense in the poem) instructions; a boy takes them to the
workmen, who are just in the act of giving their mules orders to
start pulling the wagons. Then the speaker intercedes to question
the validity of their actions and those of their ancestors: "Say, did
your fathers cross the dry Sierras/ To build another London?/ Do
Americans always have to be second-rate?" One of the workmen
speaks, concluding the second part: "San Francisco/ Is a city second only to Paris."

The physical destruction of the city and its subsequent rebuild-
ing in the image, the speaker fears, of London and Paris are

analogous to the "Unbuilding" of American in "Walt Whitman
at Bear Mountain." The speaker of "Lines Written near San
Francisco" realizes, however, that his pleas will go unheeded, for
"(Already they have nailed rough boards together)" and "(The
mortal sets—banks are the first to stand)." Thus San Francisco
will be a new mirror to reflect the Old World and to reflect
"banks," symbolic of American materialism.

Suitably, Part III is a lament for the real and symbolical "end
of America." The vigor of the language and the insistent rhythms
of the first two parts give way to quiet and somber reflec-
tion and exposition, exemplified in this stanza, despite the ex-
clamation mark: "Every night, at the end of America/ We taste
our wine, looking at the Pacific./ How sad it is, the end of America!" The speaker then brings in "cheap housing in the valleys,"
"banks [that] thrive," and the "realtors," who appear in both "In
California" and "Walt Whitman at Bear Mountain." Nonetheless,
the unsettling of the city by earth tremors still is "in the air," and
"Out there on the Pacific/ There's no America but the Marines."
It is difficult for a nation "programmed for empire" to relinquish
its momentum.

With the loss of the frontier and with the retention of the
American need to move forward, there is nowhere to go but inward. Still, the bankers and realtors have cause to rejoice; for
they are able to subdivide the valleys and mountains, to parti-
tion the continent. Their inward continent is physical, not spiritual; but Simpson's is inward: "Whitman was wrong about the
People,/ But right about himself. The land is within./ At the end
of the open road we come to ourselves." By coming "to ourselves,"
the speaker means that, since we no longer have land to pioneer—
land which both uses and satisfies our physical needs—we must
turn inward; we must examine our spiritual resources; we must,
in effect, identify and analyze our values; for now we have no
excuse (a physical entity) to delay doing so.

The image "colonists of Death" in Part III sets the foreboding
tone on which this poem and the volume end. Americans are
"colonists of Death" because of several interrelated factors with
which Simpson has been working in the four California-Whitman
poems: (1) materialistic forces, symbolized in the figures of realtors, bankers, and the like, are constructing the wrong temples
and altars ("In California," "Walt Whitman at Bear Mountain,"

"Pacific Ideas—a Letter to Walt Whitman," and "Lines Written near San Francisco"); (2) we cannot adjust to our now nonexistent physical frontier and cannot come to terms with our own inward resources, if, indeed, we have the *right* resources ("In California" and "Lines Written near San Francisco"); (3) we have deceived ourselves into thinking that from the beginning of our country we held and could fulfill great promises ("Walt Whitman at Bear Mountain" and "Lines Written near San Francisco"); (4) we are so caught up in historical emulation of great societies that we are deaf to our own sounds ("Walt Whitman at Bear Mountain," "Pacific Ideas—a Letter to Walt Whitman" and "Lines Written near San Francisco"). Thus our promise is Death, "the land/ The pioneers looked for"; our "pioneers" shaded "their eyes/ Against the sun—a murmur of serious life"; and we follow in their steps, believe the same lies, and are passing them on to our children.

Several of Simpson's poems having to do with America remain, one of which, "The Marriage of Pocahontas," is decidedly inferior and should receive little notice. The others—"On the Lawn at the Villa," "In the Suburbs," "The Redwoods," "A Farm in Minnesota," "The Inner Part," "There Is," and "Moving the Walls"—are important not only because they elucidate the poet's attitudes toward America but because they are, in addition, stylistically superior poems.

"On the Lawn at the Villa" does open with an allusion to Walt Whitman, but he is not a dominant or directional force in the poem:

> On the lawn at the villa—
> That's the way to start, eh, reader?
> We know where we stand—somewhere expensive—
> You and I *imperturbes,* as Walt would say,
> Before the diversions of wealth, you and I *engagés.*

Whitman's poem "Me Imperturbe" contains this line: "Me imperturbe standing at ease in Nature."

Since "On the Lawn at the Villa" refers to itself as a poem and thus mocks itself, it could perhaps be classified as an antipoem. But the irony implicit in the poem goes much deeper than that; the poem is a bitter indictment of "being an American":

> It's complicated, being an American,
> Having the money and the bad conscience, both at the same time.
> Perhaps, after all, this is not the right subject for a poem.

The reasons underlying this prosy bitterness are suggested in the basic situation of the poem. The speaker, an American visiting Tuscany, meets "On the lawn at the villa" "a manufacturer of explosives,/ His wife from Paris,/ And a young man named Bruno." Because the speaker is an American and thus "somehow superior," he is willing to talk to these "malefactors"; and by "superior," the speaker tells us he means "democratic." His anger, then, is directed not only toward himself as an American but also toward the Italian owner of the villa and his entourage; for all of them, by their presence at the villa, itself a symbol of wealth, are contributing to the "diversions of wealth" which must be held accountable for much of the world's ills, material and otherwise.

This strange poem concludes with these understated, ironic lines:

> We were all sitting there paralyzed
> In the hot Tuscan afternoon,
> And the bodies of the machine-gun crew were draped
>   over the balcony.
> So we sat there all afternoon.

The specific motivations for the conditions of the scene described —the American at the villa, the dead machine-gun crew—is never explained; for "On the Lawn at the Villa" is a Surrealistic interpretation of the bitter feelings the speaker holds about "being an American." At least the other players in this drama, including the bodies of the machine-gun crew, belong where they are; but the speaker does not. Even though the manufacturer, his wife, and Bruno are, like the speaker, spiritually dead ("paralyzed"), they have a right to be where they are. "On the Lawn at the Villa" is, in summary, the Surrealistic equivalent of an emotion felt by the speaker; the emotion is guilt for "being an American," for feeling "superior" to the rest of the world, and for participating in the "diversions of wealth." [12]

Another curious yet fascinating poem is the six-line "In the Suburbs":

> There's no way out.
> You were born to waste your life.
> You were born to this middleclass life
>
> As others before you
> Were born to walk in procession
> To the temple, singing.

The tone of indictment in the first three lines is mitigated by the analogy in the last three. Certainly Americans who lead ritualistic lives in the suburbs have good-paying jobs, long-term mortages, wives active in civic affairs, scrubbed and achieving children, friendly dogs, and so on. But they are not to blame, for their rut was grooved by the wheels of every preceding civilization.

The American middle class, the suburbanites, is also the subject of "The Inner Part," a poem which by metaphor rather than by statement affirms Simpson's beliefs about America expressed in the California-Whitman poems. Since much of the satiric thrust of "The Inner Part" relies on rhythm and since the effect of the closing metaphor depends on a cumulative set of conditions, I am reproducing the entire poem:

> When they had won the war
> And for the first time in history
> Americans were the most important people—
>
> When the leading citizens no longer lived in their shirt sleeves,
> And their wives did not scratch in public;
> Just when they'd stopped saying "Gosh!"—
>
> When their daughters seemed as sensitive
> As the tip of a fly rod,
> And their sons were as smooth as a V-8 engine—
>
> Priests, examining the entrails of birds,
> Found the heart misplaced, and seeds
> As black as death, emitting a strange odor.

Yohma Gray makes some interesting observations on "The Inner Part": "In this poem the shift from the naive buoyancy of pre-World War I America to the sophisticated despair of post-World War I America conveys, as a prose paraphrase cannot, a sense of the exchange of innocence for the knowledge of good and evil. The oblique reference to classical civilization ominously suggests the inevitable consequence of that knowledge, death. Ironically, it prophesies World War II." [13] The "exchange of innocence for the knowledge of good and evil" is a point interestingly taken, and death certainly is the "inevitable consequence of that knowledge"—at least in light of Simpson's "colonists of Death" concept of Americans. The "seeds," then, would be a metaphor for the foundations upon which this country was built originally and continued to grow. Simpson echoes his belief that the American need for dominance and superiority will be a factor responsible for its eventual destruction. The "heart misplaced" could be read as part of the same metaphor, emphasizing that the concepts inherent in the American Dream were erroneous to start with, an idea found in both "Walt Whitman at Bear Mountain" and "Lines Written near San Francisco."

Although Simpson's recent poetry is moving, as he says, out away from the city, two poems—"Summer Morning" and "There Is"—from *At the End of the Open Road* deal explicitly, though not exclusively, with the city. The former has been treated earlier in Section II of this chapter. The latter is a three-part, introspective lyric touching upon but not positing the poet's stance toward America. The speaker draws the reader into the poem immediately:

> Look! From my window there's a view
> of city streets
> where only lives as dry as tortoises
> can crawl—the Gallapagos of desire.

He continues in this dramatic manner through the second stanza by calling attention to phenomena he considers microcosmic of an unsettled society: "Negroes with red hair"; "insane women on the subway"; "the word Trieste"; and "the blind man with the electric guitar." In closing Part I, the speaker confesses that he has "no profession" and that he reads the want ads: "Surely there is a secret/ which, if I knew it, would change everything!" If the speaker's appraisal of conditions in New York City is objectively valid, then the time assuredly is out of joint. So is the speaker as he mocks himself through romantic irony, recognizing at once his own problem and yet rationalizing it and himself at the same time.

The same self-deprecating attitude continues through the second section of the poem, beginning with this telling stanza:

> I have the poor man's nerve-tic, irony.
> I see through the illusions of the age!
> The bell tolls, and the hearse advances,
> and the mourners follow, for my entertainment.

I am reminded here, to an extent, of Edwin Arlington Robinson's "Miniver Cheevy" and of the first part of Ezra Pound's "Hugh Selwyn Mauberley," for in both poems the protagonists are men displaced in modern society. Both Cheevy and Mauberley, it has been argued, are masks for their respective poets. I am reminded, too, of T. S. Eliot's "The Love Song of J. Alfred Prufrock," in which Prufrock, perhaps a mask for Eliot, is another ill-fitting twentieth-century man. Like the speaker of "There Is," Prufrock is an urban dweller who mocks his own inadequacies. The references in Simpson's "There Is" to irony and to the speaker's ability (at least he hopes so) to see "through the illusions of the age" suggest that he is a poet, a conclusion reinforced by the "no profession" allusion. In any event, the speaker is probably Simpson himself.

As Part II progresses through the three remaining four-line stanzas, the speaker continues to chronicle his search for himself and for values to which he can hold. Confronted by mannequins that stare scornfully at him while they pretend "all day to be in earnest," the speaker asks: "And can it be that love is an illusion?" Part II concludes with the speaker's begging the question somewhat:

> When darkness falls on the enormous street
> the air is filled with Eros, whispering.
> Eyes, mouths, contrive to meet
> in silence, fearing they may be prevented.

The concluding section of "There Is" is a lament not only for the speaker's seemingly futile search for himself and values, but also, for other Americans whose lives are now empty:

> O businessmen like ruins,
> bankers who are Bastilles,
> widows, sadder than the shores of lakes,
> then you were happy, when you still could tremble!
>
> But all night long my window
> sheds tears of light.
> I seek the word. The word is not forthcoming.
> O syllables of light . . . O dark cathedral . . .

The techniques of the Emotive Imagination are actively working in these dramatically impressive stanzas. The metaphoric referents for the businessmen, bankers, and widows engage both our
imaginations and sympathies. We feel their losses now that they
are unable to tremble, unable to feel the exhilarations of promises
that need fulfilling. They received what they wanted, and there
is nothing left for them. The line "widows, sadder than the shores
of lakes" is especially moving. We can almost hear the water lap-
ping sadly, its force spent on the "shores of lakes." When the
focus shifts in the final stanza to the speaker himself, the emotional intensity is heightened. The religious imagery may or may
not refer explicitly to religion as such; nevertheless, the imagery
conveys the speaker's need for an experience that will be religious
in nature if not in fact.

The stanza employs contrasting images of light and dark. Night
is the physical as well as spiritual setting. The brilliant personification of the window shedding "tears of light" prepares us for
the inner drama of the closing two lines. The "word" the
speaker seeks is expressed metaphorically by light imagery, which
stands for understanding, meaning, and values and which, then,
is antithetical to the image of the night and the "dark cathedral."
The "syllables of light" are the words of knowledge, which, perhaps, come through poetry. The "dark cathedral" is the entity im-
prisoning the "light." In "Walt Whitman at Bear Mountain," the
word *cathedral* occurs in this context: "The castles, the prisons,
the cathedrals/ Unbuilding, and roses/ Blossoming from the
stones that are not there. . . ." The suggestion that *cathedral*
stands symbolically for America is, I think, a tenable one. In the
context of "There Is," the word *cathedral* might then refer to the
negative power force that America exerts over the people; but it
could also refer to the darkness of spiritual self within the

speaker. In any case, the emotive meaning of the final stanza seems clear enough: the speaker and his country need grace, but grace is not forthcoming.

"The Redwoods" and "A Farm in Minnesota," and especially the second poem, exemplify Simpson's growing interest in rural subjects. Although his commitment to images from rural America does not approach that of William Stafford, James Wright, and Robert Bly, poets with whose styles he shares affinities, Simpson's use of the outdoors in these poems is superb. "The Redwoods" is a perfect poem; for diction, images, rhythm, structure—everything is right. This kind of lyric is surely a rarity, for it is one in which the critical reader wants to change nothing. The poem is organic in the most meaningful sense of the word.

"The Redwoods" is a panegyric spoken by and about the trees, which, unlike mountains and rivers—their natural counterparts in significance—are unable to move after they reach maturity. But this stillness, this fixation to the land, does not preclude them from having "thoughts of giants—/ clouds, and at night the stars." They are rightly majestic and so "have names—gutteral, grotesque—/ Hamet, Og—names with no syllables." Yet they are vulnerable: mice gnaw at their roots; they are "too slow for death, and change/ to stone. Or else too quick,/ like candles in a fire." Like the speaker of "There Is," the redwoods need and are waiting; but, unlike him, they are neither self-deprecating nor frenetic. Rather, the redwoods are stately and dignified; thus the diction and rhythms they deserve are properly majestic, a quality especially evident as the poem closes.

"A Farm in Minnesota" is similar to both "There Is" and "The Redwoods" in that the speaker is confronted with a specific problem. In this case, the speaker is "we," the collective voice of farmers in Minnesota whose lands are unable to provide them with an adequate livelihood and whose "children . . . prefer a modern house." Like "There Is" and "The Redwoods," the poem stresses the qualities of destruction and endurance. The corn the farmers hope to harvest is subject to the debilitating whims of nature:

> The corn rows walk the earth,
> crowding like mankind between the fences,
> feeding on sun and rain;
> are broken down by hail,
> or perish of incalculable drought.

The personification in the first line and the simile in the second one give the corn a sense of identity by which the farmers have come to know it. This identity is clarified by the military terminology in the following stanza:

> And we who tend them
> from the ground up—lieutenants
> of this foot cavalry, leaning on fences
> to watch our green men never move an inch—
> who cares for us?

The answer comes in the last of this four stanza poem. But before this, the farmers' voice tells us of beds being "sold at auction," of Bibles and swords bequeathed to children who care nothing for life on a farm. The flesh of these farmers "has been consumed/ only to make more lives." But after death they will enter into the kingdom of heaven and be received with honor and respect. The same dignity in the closing lines of "The Redwoods" characterizes the final stanza of "A Farm in Minnesota":

> But when our heads are planted
> under the church, from those empty pods
> we rise in the fields of death,
> and are gathered by angels,
> and shine in the hands of God.

Unlike most of Simpson's American poems, "The Redwoods" and "A Farm in Minnesota" do not emphasize through irony those elements in this country that are decidedly negative. Of course, the redwoods, corn, and farmers are subject to neglect, a contributing factor to their eventual destruction; but they also possess endurance—the ability to withstand—and thus triumph to some degree, though, by the American material yardstick, they must be considered failures. Like the country store owner, "the housewife who knows she'd dumb,/ And the earth," the redwoods, corn, and farmers "are relieved"; they have not contracted "American dreams."

In my 1965 review of *At the End of the Open Road,* I argue that two of Simpson's longer poems—"Moving the Walls" and "The Marriage of Pocahontas"—are dull. I remain with my initial appraisal of the eleven-page "The Marriage of Pocahontas," even though the closing section, entitled "A Dream in the Woods of Virginia," is interesting. Simpson chose not to include this poem in *Selected Poems*, and I prefer to pass over it here. "Moving the Walls," however, is richer than I first thought. Only the final six lines of the poem actively introduce the subject of America, but it is implicitly the poet's concern throughout the poem.

Here is a summary, divided into the parts, of the narrative: (1) The Prince of Monaco before World War I decided to furnish his yacht, the *Hirondelle*, with oceanographic equipment to set out exploring the mysteries of the sea. Ironically, the narrator says: "There was also a whaleboat/ And a whole crew of harpooners." (2) The *Hirondelle* went on its journey; everything was recorded in the log by the Prince, who found great joy in the wonders of nature. But the expedition was incredibly naïve. (3) The yacht returned to Monaco, bringing the Prince back to the social whirl he had hoped to escape by taking the *Hirondelle* out in the first place. Relics collected from the Adventure—"A walking stick made from the backbone of a shark," coral, seashells, and the like —were placed into the museum the Prince had specifically built for that purpose. The narrative proper ends here, for the two remaining parts are the narrator's interpetation of the meaning that the Prince's voyage and return have on our lives now.

C. B. Cox has made an interesting and comprehensive analysis of "Moving the Walls." [13] He sees, for example, the opening section as "delightfully ironic": "Like the *Hirondelle*, the swallow, the Prince will only skim the surface. A dilettante, he treats Nature as a plaything, and is untouched by the hidden power of the sea, the great flood of archetypal experience. To Cox, the strange allusion to the whaleboat and harpooners is a "satire of aristocrats, indulging their fancies just before the outbreak of European war and Communist Revolution, [which] is linked with ironic treatment of the pretence that reason and science can control and finally comprehend the universe." The voyage itself, Cox maintains, is an attempt to gain "the unreachable limits of human apprehension. . . . But soon the Prince's playing at exploration is contrasted with the mysteries of the bottomless sea; like the rationalist, he is trying to understand the unfathomable."

Cox offers additional analyses of the specifics in Part 2 of the poem that relate the experiences of the sailors to both their basic inability to understand the sea and to their instinctive success, at the same time, to "step out of human limitations to become, for a brief space, involved with the mysteries of Nature." Cox continues that the gist of Part III is that the museum stands for the Prince's attempt, based on the "life of reason," to reduce "the underwater life to mundane, everyday articles." But two images act to qualify the Prince's success—indeed, the success of anyone who believes it is possible to adhere completely to the "life of reason," the closing words of Part III. As Cox explains the images, "the tearing out of the 'strange heart of the ship' and the 'red holes In the deck that vanished in smoke' suggest that some explosive force has existed in the laboratory. Beneath the surface of pre-1914 aristocratic society waited the horrors of Verdun and Passchendaele, the knowledge of evil and death which the Prince preferred to ignore."

The moral the narrator reads into the events that transpired is contained, according to Cox, in Parts IV and V: "Today we continue to evade the destructive element, to impose secure dimensions on the 'mud-clouded wars of the ocean floor.' The great epic heroes discovered themselves by their explorations, joined themselves to the hugeness of Nature. Perhaps America may repeat those epic journeys, moving the walls outwards, embracing the mysteries of the depths. But in the last stanza the poem turns round on itself."

The two stanzas closing the poem relate the American need to expand in light of the heroic adventures that the narrator talks of in earlier portions of the fifth section. But these final stanzas question seriously the value of America's expansive methods and directions, thus bringing to mind the California-Whitman poems. Although our pioneering efforts into outer space, our "branching among the stars," represent a moving of the walls, the narrator can find nothing to applaud in the way our walls are moving. We have no one at sea, no one to yield himself "To the currents that moved from within." We have no heroes and no heroic pursuits.

IV   *From Memory*

Until *At the End of the Open Road*, Louis Simpson's poems have had little to do with his family, either past or present. However, three poems—"The Troika," "A Story About Chicken Soup," and "My Father in the Night Commanding No"—from the Pulitzer volume exemplify a growing interest in this new area of inquiry, which has since 1963 been occupying a good deal of his energy, and which finds significant expression in a number of poems from *Adventures of the Letter I*, published in 1971 by Oxford University Press in London. These poems concern Simpson's real and imagined relatives from around the area of Lutsk, from which his mother's family came.

Both "The Troika" and "A Story About Chicken Soup" are structured by a curious combination of narrative sequence and image. The speaker of "The Troika" is having a dream that progressively turns into a nightmare, and it is reasonable to assume that Simpson is the speaker. Though the father alluded to in the poem could not physically be the Jamaican lawyer, he could be the emotional equivalent of the poet's father. The poem fuses together, by a series of images, incidents in Simpson's life and incidents in the lives of his ancestors whom, of course, he never knew in person.

The ordering device of "The Troika" must be the speaker's dream, which involves an imaginary ride on a troika drawn by three white horses. The sleigh and horses, the speaker says, belong to his father. As the troika speeds at night through a forest and into a small settlement, the speaker glimpses two old men, "Where lamplight like a knife/ gleams through a door," who are bending over, apparently playing a game of chess. One of the men rises, as if he might hear the spirit of the speaker passing by in the night. But the speaker is unable to stop; in fact, he whips the horses on into

>   fields
> littered with debris. And there in trenches
> the guardsmen stand, wind fluttering their rags.
>
> And there were darker fields without a moon.
> I walk across a field, bound on an errand.
> The errand's forgotten—something depended on it.
> A nightmare! I have lost my father's horses!

The scenes described above are fields of war: the first, a scene from World War I in which, the speaker imagines, his ancestors in the old country participated; the second, the "darker fields" and the field walked across, is from Simpson's experiences as a runner in World War II in the European theater. Thus personal family history becomes confused in the dream with World War II, which itself becomes the nightmare of having lost the horses.

The speaker shifts tenses repeatedly in "The Troika," lending credibility to the fact of the dream. For example, he tells of a white bird that "rises/ and goes before me, hopping through the forest." Then he "held the bird—it vanished with a cry," after which he comes upon a girl with black hair who "sat sideways" on a branch: "The dew/ shone on her lips; her breasts were white as roses." Perhaps the bird is the metamorphosed Heinrich in "The Bird"; perhaps the girl is the one who came in a vision to Dodd in "The Runner."

The use of ellipses in the following two lines suggests that the dream-become-nightmare has finally come to an end, which is affirmed by the speaker's repossession of the horses he said he lost: "Troika, troika! Three white horses,/ a whip of silver, and my father's sleigh. . . ." The closing stanza is lyrically antipodal to the stark, jolting lines that precede:

> When morning breaks, the sea
> gleams through the branches,
> and the white bird, enchanted,
> is flying through the world, across the sea.

White is the dominant and ordering color of "The Troika": the ground is covered with snow; the moon is shining; the three horses are white; the breasts of the girl "were white as roses"; and the bird is white (the tense irregularities are Simpson's). The white bird of "The Troika," instead of Heinrich's bird, is a dove, a symbol of peace; and it symbolizes in the poem the peace within himself which the speaker achieves the morning following the dream-nightmare. Since the dove is flying "across the sea," there is a suggestion that the speaker hopes for peace throughout the world.

"The Troika," then, is a symbolic dream odyssey backward in time through Simpson's European heritage and his experiences as a soldier in World War II. The poem is also exemplary of his new imagination and techniques. The structure of the poem is a seeming irrationality, a leaping out beyond the boundaries of reality into fantasy, a series of epiphanies. "The Troika" reveals the "drama and narrative of the subconscious." "The images move,

with the logic of dreams," as Simpson writes in 1966 concerning
the task of the Surrealistic poet.

"A Story About Chicken Soup" is divided into three brief seg-
ments, and the narration is united by the effects that the incidents
in the first two sections have on the speaker as he tries to come
to terms with his past and present in the third section of the poem.
As in "The Troika," the speaker's heritage and remembered past
play significant roles. The narrative begins, therefore, with a dis-
arming description of life in the house of the speaker's grandmother, who apparently lived in America. At her house, the
speaker recalls, there was always chicken soup and talk of life in
the old country, good times and bad. On occasion, the grandmother sent a dowry to a bride in Poland: "Imagine/ The rice-
powdered faces!/ And the smell of the bride, like chicken soup."
There is an abrupt change in tone and subject, for the speaker's
ancestors were of Jewish extraction: "But the Germans killed
them./ I know it's in bad taste to say it,/ But it's true. The
Germans killed them all."

In the next section (parts in this poem are divided by asterisks,
not numbers), the subject shifts to the ruins of Berchtesgaden,[14]
where, as the speaker remembers, a little German girl, "all skin
and bones," was hiding. This shift from German atrocities to a
German civilian casualty documents Simpson's belief that war
leaves no one untouched. The little girl, whose "mechanical
brothers" were killed by the American soldiers with whom she
comes to laugh, was, the speaker comments ironically, forgiven
her sin of being a German by the Americans.

The final section of "A Story About Chicken Soup" takes place in
the present and is a meditation about the events of the preceding
sections. The irony is gone; the tone is sober, reflective. The characters have long disappeared, yet they still exert demands on the
speaker:

> They want me to stick in their mudhole
> Where no one is elegant.
> They want me to wear old clothes,
> They want me to be poor, to sleep in a room with many others—
>
> Not to walk in the painted sunshine
> To a summer house,
> But to live in the tragic world forever.

It is difficult, indeed impossible, to extricate guilt completely. The guilt the speaker feels is personal only to the extent that by heritage and participation he had been made aware of a world outside of America in which "sunshine" and summer houses are symbolically absent. The "painted sunshine" is probably a metaphor for California, which has real and "painted" (imposed) "sunshine" (happiness). The "summer house," probably the second and small house on Simpson's property in Berkeley where he spent his mornings writing, represents symbolically the wealth, the pleasure, and the other things affluence can buy. But knowledge of death, violence, and poverty stays with him constantly as a reminder of the "tragic world." Apart from sympathy tempered by and expressed through irony in the first two sections, the attitude the speaker holds toward this knowledge is uncertain. The contrasting life habits create tension in the poem and in the mind of the speaker: death, violence, and poverty, on the one hand; "painted sunshine" and a "summer house" on the other. I think he will "live in the tragic world forever," at least in the tragic world of memory.

The final poem to be considered in this chapter has been cited by reviewers and critics as one of Simpson's finest poems. As I have already made clear, I share their enthusiam, for "My Father in the Night Commanding No" is exceptional. More so than any other poem to date, it draws from family experience. There is no doubt that Simpson is the speaker. With the exception of "The Riders Held Back," which is rhymed, metered, and structured by quatrains, "My Father in the Night Commanding No" is the most formally executed poem in *At the End of the Open Road*. Each of the eleven quatrains rhyme the first and fourth lines. The meter approaches iambic, with the first, second, and fourth lines having basically five beats; the second line, two beats. Despite these external regulations, the imagination behind the poem is charged and exciting. Diction, rhythms, and images are exact as well as evocative.

In the opening quatrains, the speaker recalls an evening at home in his childhood, an evening, we can assume, that was more typical than special:

> My father in the night commanding No
> Has work to do. Smoke issues from his lips;

He reads in silence.
The frogs are croaking and the streetlamps glow.

And then my mother winds the gramophone;
The Bride of Lammermoor begins to shriek—
Or reads a story
About a prince, a castle, and a dragon.

In the autobiographical essays "Confessions of an American Poet"
and "The Marriage of Scotland and Poland," Simpson tells of his
father, whose concerns were practical, and of his mother, whose
interests were imaginative. She told Simpson and his older brother
Herbert of life in Poland, read them romances, and was devoted
to opera; therefore the night of the first two stanzas must have
been enacted many times. It is interesting that the speaker uses
the present tense to describe the events of this night and that the
voice of the speaker is the voice of a child. Frogs croaking and
streetlamps glowing are things a child would notice. The word
shriek and the phraseology of "story/ About a prince, a castle, and
a dragon" suggest a child's manner of apprehending.

Then the speaker announces that the excitement of which his
mother read and the gramophone shrieked has indeed come true,
for he has been to Thule, Paris, Venice, Rome, and has experienced "The journey and the danger of the world." Abruptly, as if
in a dream, the scene shifts; for in the sixth quatrain, which is the
exact middle of the poem, we have the speaker as a father himself
coming home from work to find his children not at all surprised:
"They were expecting me."

In the five quatrains that remain, the speaker seeks to understand his parents, who still remain "on the stage of terror and of
love" (they were divorced when Simpson was about seven years
old). Although he "once pretended/ To understand them," he
knews he never did or will. The three of them—father, mother, son
—seem like actors in a playhouse, puppets with wooden heads.
The poem concludes with these emotively alive lines:

Father, why did you work? Why did you weep,
Mother? Was the story so important?
"*Listen!*" the wind
Said to the children, and they fell asleep.

By "commanding No," the father broke lines of communication between himself and the rest of the family, including his wife, who probably suffered more than anyone else. The only communication within the family came through the mother—stories, operas—and these, of course, hardly matter as communication. The wind that ends the poem appears also in the seventh stanza in this way: "And the dark wind/ Is murmuring that nothing ever happens." Thus the wind is a means of communication; it whispers to the boys at the end to *"Listen"* to sounds it brings from the larger world outside, the one that the Gramophone shrieked and the mother talked about and that the speaker experienced in his journeys. And yet his father and mother bother him; he is so inexorably a part of them that it is impossible to escape their presence. Therefore *At the End of the Open Road*, apart from its singular excellence, serves to introduce readers to something of Simpson's personal life —a subject he continues to use as material for significant poems.

CHAPTER 6

Selected Poems

IN 1965, Harcourt, Brace & World issued the *Selected Poems* of Louis Simpson; and it included three poems from *The Arrivistes*, fifteen from *Good News of Death and Other Poems*, seventeen from *A Dream of Governors*, twenty-four from *At the End of the Open Road*, and twelve new poems. The three from *The Arrivistes*—"Carentan O Carentan," "Summer Storm," and "Song: 'Rough Winds Do Shake the Darling Buds of May' "—are the best of his early work; in fact, as I have stated elsewhere, "Carentan O Carentan" is his finest war poem and one of his best lyrics. The poems omitted from the four previous volumes must have been those Simpson considered the weaker ones. For example, the pastoral, "Good News of Death," and the narrative, "The Marriage of Pocahontas," are both absent. Of the twelve poems constituting the "New Poems" section, at least one, "Columbus," was written prior to the 1963 publication of *At the End of the Open Road*; for it first appeared in the May 27, 1961 issue of the *New Yorker*. Since "Columbus" is rhymed, metered, and rather fluidly examines the subject of America, its exclusion from the Pulitzer volume is understandable. It does not invite favorable comparison with the California-Whitman poems or with the additional America poems of that collection.

I *The Method*

Excluding "Columbus," the diction and rhythms of the New Poems are distinctly colloquial. The techniques of the Emotive Imagination, the means by which Louis Simpson has come to embody Surrealism, are thoroughly woven into the fabric of these poems. Before I consider "The Tailor's Wedding," a splendid poem that walks delicately the border between the real and imaginary, I want to discuss "Tonight the Famous Psychiatrist" and "Out-

ward," both exemplary, as far as any poems can be, of the two
related methods Simpson is using in his recent poems.

"Tonight the Famous Psychiatrist" is the kind of poem in which
Simpson lets the situation speak for itself. We learn from statement after statement that a party given by the famous psychiatrist
is attended by celebrities, by "flesh-colored girls," and by "figures
from the sporting world." And, too, there are a liberal Jew and a
Negro who laughs "like a trumpet." There is little doubt that the
host is eminently successful until it is revealed in the closing lines
that his wife is mentally ill:

> The wife of the host enterly slowly.
> Poor woman!
> She thinks she is still in Hungary,
> And clings to her knitting needles.
> For her the time passes slowly.

"Tonight the Famous Psychiatrist" is a sober instance of the understated rhythms (punctuated by "Poor woman!") that charac-
terize Simpson's poems since 1959. The lines are conversational
yet insistent.

"Outward" is rhythmically similar but differs significantly from
"Tonight the Famous Psychiatrist" in its reliance on images and its
typical use of the more startling qualities of the Emotive Imagination. "Outward" is important enough to reproduce in full:

> The staff slips from the hand
> Hissing and swims on the polished floor.
> It glides away to the desert.
>
> It floats like a bird or lily
> On the waves, to the ones who are arriving.
> And if no god arrives,
>
> Then everything yearns outward.
> The honeycomb cell brims over
> And the atom is broken in light.
>
> Machines have made their god. They walk or fly.
> The towers bend like Magi, mountains weep,
> Needles go mad, and metal sheds a tear.

*

> The astronaut is lifted
> Away from the world, and drifts.
> How easy it is to be there!
>
> How easy to be anyone, anything but oneself!
> The metal of the plane is breathing;
> Sinuously it swims through the stars.

The personifications, the series of juxtaposed images, the metaphoric leaps, and the unusual ending all speak of the new reaches of Simpson's imagination. Of course, the structure of the poem up to the asterisk break seems irrational; the content is elusive, and the confusing images strike one after another. The meaning of the poem as a whole, however, is clear enough if only the closing six lines are considered: an astronaut is in outer space, which leads the speaker to conclude that self-knowledge is more difficult to achieve than that of how "to be anyone, anything. . . ."

By metaphoric extension, title relevance, and the materialistic stress in the first four stanzas, we are led to conclude that "Outward" is another Simpson statement about the American need to expand and about the difficulty the country has in achieving honest introspection. So "Outward," in a sense, is a companion poem to the four California-Whitman poems from *At the End of the Open Road*. But it is also different; for, while the California-Whitman poems are explicitly about America, "Outward" is implicitly about the country. On a literal level, the closing lines of the poem relate to personal, not national, self-knowledge—a thematic consideration of "Stumpfoot on 42nd Street," which is discussed later in this chapter.

More interesting than thematic objects is the imaginative and imagistic structuring of "Outward." The subject-verb constructions in the poem create conversational rhythms out of images that would hardly appear in anyone's conversation; there is tension generated by the opposites of a quiet manner of presentation and the shocking quality of the images, which, one after another, confound the reader; but curiously, there is a rightness about "Outward" that the reader emotively understands.

An interesting technical phenomenon in these New Poems occurs in "The Tailor's Wedding" and "The Laurel Tree." Both poems are seventy lines long and are divided into five sections of fourteen lines each, each section consisting of four tercets and concluding with a couplet. There is neither a metrical pattern nor a rhyme scheme. Each section, however, does develop with the logic of a sonnet (like Robert Frost's "Acquainted with the Night") and is divided into four tercets rather than the three quatrains of the English sonnet scheme. "The Tailor's Wedding" is exemplary of yet another development in Simpson's new, imaginative departures. Some of the earlier poems ("I Dreamed that in a City Dark as Paris" and "The Flight to Cytherea" from *A Dream of Governors*; "The Troika" and "On the Lawn at the Villa" from *At the End of the Open Road*) are structured by dreamlike or by hallucinatory qualities, which are indicative of the poet's attempts to write Surrealistic poetry. Of course, "I Dreamed that in a City Dark as Paris" and "The Flight to Cytherea" appeared early enough in Simpson's career to raise the objection that he was not actively seeking to create the "logic of dreams." In any case, if Surrealism was not on his mind, it is in the poems.

Here is an itinerary of "The Tailor's Wedding." In the first part, the speaker, an American in Italy (not a new situation in Simpson's poetry), is having a suit of clothes altered by a tailor whose "work was perfect—and cheap, considering/ That the man's life came with it." The tailor's workroom, which was also his home, had a wall on which were hung pictures of women cut out of magazines. In the second part, the effect on the speaker of the tailor and on the condition of his life style was considerable: "The interior of the room was as clear/ As a glimpse of brain surgery." The tailor, whose craft is "cutting and stitching," becomes archetypal to the speaker: "And when I look back, the hero/ Who lifts Medusa's head/ Must yield to the tailor's scissors." The speaker is then reminded of his days as a student and of "life/ Out there— the light that hurt the eyes." Like a tailor, the speaker in those days cut and stitched

> Ideas by a dim light—
> Handwork, in an age of machinery;
>
> While the streets belonged to the rich—
> The people with strong teeth.

Thus there is a reversal of station; now the speaker, it is implied, metaphorically owns the streets and has strong teeth.

The third part of the poem digresses even more, from the life the tailor leads to the speaker's past, which was characterized by a kind of poverty. The rich, symbolically represented by "the smell of new car upholstery,/ A wind, white tablecloths," are contrasted to the poor—and specifically to the speaker in his youth who was referred to in the third person. Above the rich and poor alike, "The moon hangs, faithful to the last,/ Revealing her amorous craters." The moon then turns into the "Muse of the city, hope of the insane," without which the speaker would have been lost (here the present tense is employed; the trip backward in time has been achieved). Simpson here employs the two most common connotations of the moon: love and insanity.

In the fourth part, as we continue looking back into the life of the student, the tailor is replaced by a girl, "the household drudge" of the family with whom the student "perhaps" once roomed. She sees in the student the figure of a "hero" to whom on a cold night she can bring a bowl of soup. Love, as the third section implies, is the province of anyone, rich or poor, so the girl's fantasy is quite tenable. But the student had to leave and was therefore unable to bring lasting comfort through love to the girl, who, with a rancid and thin body, must have stood "At the door, convulsed in a handkerchief," as her hero left forever. The tailor then reappears as a likely mate for the girl; and the speaker, acting in the role of her father, gives her away in marriage: "Dear heart, I have bestowed/ Your hand on a skillful tailor." Together the tailor and the girl can erase their mutual loneliness.

In the fifth section of the poem, we must ask what of the speaker, who, in his imagination, is marriage broker, consoler of the lonely? "Lightly I've gone through life, accepting/ Their services—a soup bowl/ And a suit of clothes." His own feelings have been "left on the cutting-room floor"; but he does not despair, for he has done good things: he bought a suit of clothes from a lonely tailor; he let a "household drudge" know love for him; and, of course, he imaginatively joined them in marriage. Obviously, the speaker of "The Tailor's Wedding" feels that his life, viewed as a whole, has been something of a waste—a waste mitigated only by his good deeds. The poem concludes:

> And I've come to the end of a street
> That is full of strangers.
> And still, a spot is gleaming—

> Something like a handkerchief
> Or a pair of scissors.

This ending underscores a unique quality of "The Tailor's Wedding"; unlike Simpson's other dreamlike odysseys to date, this poem contains nothing akin to nightmare or terror. Nevertheless, its logic is structured by associations, the drama of the narrative occurring entirely in the active mind of the speaker. Its theme is compassion, sympathy, and feeling.

II *The East and The West*

Although the external forms of "The Tailor's Wedding" and "The Laurel Tree" are identical, the contextual natures are quite dissimilar. "The Laurel Tree" does, however, move with a similar dreamlike fluidity in and out of empirically defined reality; and its primary subjects are (1) our civilization has not progressed as far as we should like to believe it has and (2) the lack of communication between Eastern and Western ways of life has led to violence.

"Things," the poem following "The Laurel Tree" in *Selected Poems*, continues the dialogue for communication and meaning between the East and the West, expands on the difference between cultures, and concludes with a hopeful solution to the problems that existing barriers create. The speaker is the same individual, a representative of Western poetry, of "The Laurel Tree"; the spokesman for the East is a man who "stood in the laurel tree/ Adjusting his hands and feet to the boughs." He seems to be a "flower-child" of San Francisco, a hippie who told the speaker: "Today I was breaking stones/ On a mountain road in Asia," when he had a vision "Of mankind, like grass and flowers." To be specific and perhaps too literal, the vision, which continues as follows, "We forgave each other; we gave ourselves/ Wholly over to words," could have been induced by marijuana, "grass." In effect, and regardless of the means by which it was brought about, communication between the East (those on the mountain) and the West (the "hippie" spokesman for the East and, by implication, the speaker of the poem) was achieved; the two worlds, then, were at peace in this vision. When the speaker, whose commitments are to the West, mocked the vision of the man, he replied, "I am impervious to irony," which began an exchange of

philosophical positions. The man in the laurel tree spoke for the
world of spirit; the speaker, for materialism.

In the self-deprecating passage that follows, the speaker identifies himself as a poet. He mocks, as well, the spiritual reality of
"things" set forth by the man in the laurel tree:

> I said, "I have suspected
> The Mixmaster knows more than I do,
> The air conditioner is the better poet.
> My right front tire is as bald as Odysseus—
> How much it must have suffered!"

At the same time, the poet-speaker acknowledges the need to listen to both philosophies, as "Things" concludes on this prescriptive
note:

> "Then, as things have a third substance
> Which is obscure to both our senses,
> Let there be a perpetual coming and going
> Between your house and mine."

III *America Once More*

Both "The Laurel Tree" and "Things" point to a new area of
inquiry for Louis Simpson. Moving beyond the physical boundaries of America, he considers the American spirit as it exists in
opposition to that of the East. His discovery that the cultures are
innately antithetical is hardly new knowledge, but his method in
these poems is, to an extent, new for him. This method involves a
kind of rational Surrealism, to which the techniques of the Emotive Imagination are ideally suited. The New Poems from *Selected
Poems*, however, do not all represent a moving outward from the
American continent. Four poems—"Black Kettle Raises the Stars
and Stripes," [1] "After Midnight," "The Union Barge on Staten Island," and "Stumpfoot on 42nd Street"—are defined within the
physical continent; and the most interesting of these poems is
"Stumpfoot on 42nd Street." The nature of reality and a man's
sense of personal identity are the subjects of the curious poem
"Stumpfoot on 42nd Street," which could be read as a series of
images aiming at a definition of what it means to be an American.
Stumpfoot is a Negro who "sprouts from the pavement like an
asparagus" and who beats a drum and symbol and plays a trumpet.

Stumpfoot is, as the title denotes, physically deformed. Although
the poem places him squarely within an American context of flag
waving and poverty, the content is not so much about Stumpfoot
and his country as about what it means to be a person, a human
being, an entity. The image of Stumpfoot playing musical instru-
ments on the street with a tin cup occupies the first of this three-
part poem and is done extremely well. Stumpfoot, we are told by
the speaker, is not embarrassed by his condition:

> It is for you to feel embarrassed,
> Or God, or the way things are.
>
> Therefore he plays the trumpet
> And therefore he beats the drum.

The speaker of the poem is someone whose thoughts stray,
whose imagination is very active, and who is made distinctly un-
comfortable by the fact of Stumpfoot. The second part begins with
the speaker's thinking of himself in Venezuela "With flowers, and
clouds in the distance," but he is abruptly brought out of his brown
study of the presence of Stumpfoot standing "near a window/ Ad-
vertising cameras, trusses, household utensils./ The billboards
twinkle. The time/ Is 12:26." The objective qualities of time,
place, and incident both repulse and infuriate the speaker:

> O why don't angels speak in the infinite
> To each other? Why this confusion,
> These particular bodies—
> Eros with clenched fists, sobbing and cursing?

In the concluding section of the poem, the mind of the speaker
again drifts to Venezuela; but since his fancy does not work, the
vision is unpleasant. The speaker visualizes himself in the jungle;
he is being eaten by ants; his "ribs are caught in a thorn bush/
And thought has no reality." Then, by means of Surrealistic association, he thinks of Stumpfoot in his meanly furnished room, un-
strapping "his apparatus," "taking off his boots," "easing his
stumps," and, finally, "lighting a cigar." The final two lines of the
poem are quiet but firmly insistent: "'It seems to say that a man
exists/ Only to say, Here I am in person."
The considerations I posed earlier of reality and identity in this

poem are working between Stumpfoot and the speaker. The reality for which Stumpfoot stands is ugly and repulsive, but the
speaker finally realizes that he cannot escape imaginatively or any
way from the Stumpfoots of the world. Rather than escaping, he
feels metaphorically through the ants in Venezuela the pain
Stumpfoot knows; the knowledge growing from his desire to escape leads him to understand that, indeed, Stumpfoot is real, a
man existing who, like everyone else, has his pleasure and his pain.
The speaker learns to do what Stumpfoot is doing, which is to accept the real for what it is and to make the best of it. Thus "Stumpfoot on 42nd Street" does seem to be more about the personal
than national situation, though the setting and situation are
ironically American.

IV *"In the Time of Villa"*

The last poem in *Selected Poems* is interesting for several reasons. First, "In the Time of Villa" is an ironic postscript to the
canon of Louis Simpson's poetry to 1965. Second, it is an ironic
commentary on the instance of his birth and on the subsequent
life he has led. Third, it is another stylistic exemplum of Simpson's use of the Emotive Imagination. The situation of the poem
concerns a man who, "in the time of [Pancho] Villa," was put on
trial to justify his existence. His accusers shouted " 'To the wall!' "
When he awoke from a state or condition unknown to the reader,
the "stars/ Were shining above the Plaza de Toros" and a "column
of ants passed by," distracted away from him "by a particle/ Coming the opposite way...." The speaker, Louis Simpson, then tells
of having

> heard some Indians talking ...
> Long ago, and yet it seems
> Like yesterday.
> And that is why, and why
>
> I live by begging.
> And it's not just for myself,
> But the head and ears of the burro
> Nodding against the stars.

"In the Time of Villa" is, of course, a metaphor that is continually expanding, contracting, and moving in multiple directions. It

seems that the "begging" is Simpson's ironic equivalent of writing poetry, for which he, as the speaker, is on trial. He is on trial, as well, for being born in the first place; and his father and mother act the roles of judge and juror in the poem. Pancho Villa died in 1923, the year of Simpson's birth, which accounts for the curious allusion in the title; but Mexican imagery continues throughout the poem as a unifying device.

The fifth line, "They were shouting 'To the wall!,' " should remind us of "The Cradle Trap" from *At the End of the Open Road,* for the situation is analogous in that an infant is being conditioned to respond to demands imposed by his parents: "They say, I love you./ They shout, You must!" The telling links in diction between the poems are provided by the pronoun *they* and by the verb forms *shouting* and *shout.* But the implications in the newer poem go beyond justification for being born; by extension, the speaker is on trial for the major force in his public life, the writing of poetry. Even when Simpson was a student at Columbia University in the early 1940's, he admitted feeling guilty about writing poetry.

The Emotive Imagination in the Villa poem is found primarily in the image associations. One image leads and leaps to another: the wall to stars to ants to Indians to a burro and, finally, to stars again. The speaker's justification for writing poetry is the gist of the closing image, an imaginative leap characteristic of those frequently marking Simpson's poems since he abandoned the conventions in favor of a new style. Here the juxtaposing of burro and stars creates the spark representative of the highly imaginative type of poetry Simpson is writing.

CHAPTER 7

Adventures of the Letter I

IN DECEMBER, 1967, Louis Simpson sent for my examination a manuscript of nineteen poems that he felt "fairly sure" would be included in *The Wall Test,* the tentative title of a volume of poetry he was then assembling. As it turned out, Simpson did include nearly everything in that manuscript; and he, of course, added a number of other poems. Of the nineteen he sent me, he eliminated one and incorporated several of the shorter pieces into longer poems. Published in 1971 by Oxford University Press in London, the volume is titled *Adventures of the Letter I.* After having rejected *The Wall Test* as a title, Simpson planned to call the collection *An American Peasant.* The title he settled on is clearly an improvement over his second choice and more indicative of the contents than the first title, which is also the name of one of the poems, a curiously forceful piece:

> When they say 'To the wall!'
> and the squad does a right turn,
>
> where do you stand? With the squad
> or the man against the wall?
>
> In every case
> you find yourself standing against the wall.

In the spring of 1969, Simpson told me that he had serious doubts about the effectiveness of "In the Time of Villa," the last poem in *Selected Poems* and the one with which my discussion in the preceding chapter closed. My comments on its values stand, and I think it appropriate for me to introduce a discussion of *Adventures of the Letter I* by reprinting "The Wall Test," not only because Simpson once considered that as the title of his collection, but because of two additional factors: (1) there is a logical progression from the speaker of "In the Time of Villa" being put on trial ("They were shouting 'To the wall!'") to this brief poem; (2) there is more personal, direct involvement between Simpson and his poems in *Adventures of the Letter I* than in his previous volumes of poetry, this involvement being nicely exampled in "The Wall Test." In *Poet's Choice*, a 1962 anthology, Simpson remarked that most of his poems derive from actual experiences.[1] No one doubts this derivation, but the feeling that the poet is speaking about an event, an incident, or the like in which he participated is present more so in these poems than in any of the other collections. At any rate, Simpson *is* speaking the poems, though I prefer to remain for the most part with calling the speaker *speaker*, not Simpson, which act allows the collateral benefit of Simpson's imagination more freedom than would a direct accounting.

The stylistic apparatus Simpson brings to these poems is similar to that discussed in the Method subdivision of the preceding chapter. The reader who has followed Simpson's work from *At the End of the Open Road* already knows what to expect: colloquial language, conversational rhythms, and alert images juxtaposed with other alert images. The imagination within the poems often seems to be irrational, a condition arising from a structure predicated on images that move with the "logic of dreams." The reader also finds that Simpson continues to remain with the subject of America, that Jamaica and his childhood emerge as subjects, that his mental confinement after World War II is now a subject, and that Simpson returns to "Troika" and "A Story About Chicken Soup"—two poems from *At the End of the Open Road*—as models for an interesting new direction in the poetry: treatments of relatives in the Old World, relatives he never knew and is never likely to know.

I *"Volhynia Province"*

The first section of *Adventures of the Letter I*, which is titled "Volhynia Province," is prefaced by the following explanation:

When I was a child we lived in a house called Volyn, after Volhynia, the part of Russia where my mother was born. Volhynia was the greatest imaginable distance from the island [Jamaica] on which we lived. It snowed a great deal in Volhynia; there were wolves, Cossacks, and gypsies.

Since then I have learned that the people of Volhynia were poor and afraid of many things. They died in epidemics, the 'Volhynia fever' for which the province is noted in medical dictionaries. Yet some of them were scholars and cigarette-smoking intellectuals.

I have come to think of the country around Lutsk, where my mother's people lived, as a muddy plain with a dismal climate. Yet recently I met a Polish drama-critic who remembered spending a fortnight on the river near Lutsk canoeing with a girl. She was dressed like a Viennese and carried a blue parasol.

A curious romantic quality about the seven poems in the Volhynia Province division makes one feel that Simpson deeply laments not having known his relatives and their lives in Lutsk. And so he tries through imaginative leaps spanning place and time to understand the humor, pathos, horror, and ordinary circumstances of life these people experienced in the time of his maternal grandmother (from whom, we can assume, he gleaned some of the subject matter) and in the case of "Dvoyna" are still experiencing. Dvoyna is a cousin twice-removed from the speaker. The first three stanzas of the poem are the speaker's dream of being with her in a garden "In the town of Odessa"; they are in love; they talk of Chekhov's plays; they drink tea. "But this is only a dream," the fourth stanza begins; and the opening line of the fifth and concluding stanza is a melancholy statement of theme: "We are only phantoms, bits of ash."

And so these poems continue in like manner: with, for example, "Avram the cello-mender,/ the only Jewish sergeant/ in the army of the Tsar" ["A Son of the Romanovs"]; with a crazy beggar who claimed, " 'I'm a natural son/ of the Grand Duke Nicholas' " ["A Son of the Romanovs"]; with Isidor, who "was always plotting/ to overthrow the government" ["Isidor"]; and with Adam Yankev, whose name tugs at Simpson's memory: "I can see my mother's family/ sitting around the kitchen stove/ arguing—the famous Russian theater" ["Adam Yankev"]. As the poem continues into the present, the speaker walks "with a head full of ancient life," but he is confronted with and confounded by the phenomena of America everywhere; and he sadly interprets: "I feel I am part of a race/ that has not yet arrived in America./ Yet, these people—their faces are strangely familiar." Despite the distances of time and space, the "voices and shadows of desire,/ and the tears of things" are

always here; we are all part of the human family: "Around us/
things want to be understood," the act of which Simpson is trying
to accomplish not only in the poems of Volhynia Province but in
his entire canon as well.

II *America*

The subject of America proper is introduced by section two, Indian Country, its title poem in three parts, one of which, "Black
Kettle Raises the Stars and Stripes," had appeared earlier in the
New Poems division of *Selected Poems*. Simpson's only earlier
treatment of the American Indian is his narrative already discussed "The Marriage of Pocahontas" included in *At the End of
the Open Road*. The point of the "Indian Country" trilogy is an
old one: the Indians were badly mistreated. It is, however, of interest to note that Simpson's dictions and rhythms in this poem
seem remarkably close to those of William Stafford, who has
written some fine lyrics on the Indians.

The title, Indian Country, refers as well to America; and with
"The Climate of Paradise" and the subsequent poems of this section, Simpson moves into the subject with which he has had the
most success in his poetry: analyses of American life. In this section, Simpson also returns to the subject of war, a familiar one
from his first volume on; but his treatment now is decidedly different: he is no longer interested in the individual soldier or in the
absurd ways in which war is conducted; rather, he uses war in the
context of a haunting consciousness. "The Climate of Paradise,"
for example, begins by alluding to Indians who once laid claim to
Mount Shasta; and then the poem proceeds to contrast the concept of Indian gods inhabiting the mountain with American citi-
zens who are "haunted by Red China—/ bugles—a sky lit with
artillery." Structurally, Simpson uses the governing metaphor of
caves: (1) those in which the Indian gods lived; (2) the "imposing villas" of Pasadena; (3) the caves in which Vico said thought
begins; and (4) the recesses of the mind: "O even in Paradise/ the
mind would make its own winter."

The America of California, a subject explored brilliantly in *At
the End of the Open Road*, figures significantly in "On the Eve,"
in which war again appears in a haunting capacity. The poem begins, in fact, as if it were included in *At the End of the Open*

Road: "There is something sad about property/ where it ends, in California." We are reminded particularly of this stanza from "Lines Written near San Francisco": "Every night, at the end of America/ We taste our wine, looking at the Pacific./ How sad it is, the end of America!" Another sequence from the poem is especially interesting in light of the poem "Cristina," which first appeared in *The Distinctive Voice*, a 1966 anthology. In "Cristina," a love lyric with a metaphorically exciting ending, the last three lines are: "I move on the ocean floor./ I stamp on the ooze of the ocean floor/ While light floats on the surface." Though used in a different context, a revised version of these lines closes the second part of "On the Eve":

> Lifting their heavy arms and feet
>
> they stamp on the ocean floor.
> They rise from the ooze of the ocean floor
> to the lights that float on the surface.

In "Cristina," the lines surrealistically represent the emotions of the speaker, who is in love with the girl. In "On the Eve," they Surrealistically represent the emotions of the "businessman of San Francisco" in response to topless "go-go" girls. "On the Eve" ends with an allusion to the war in Vietnam, illustrating once again the poet's use of war in an ominous, haunting context: "and ships, wrapped in a mist,/ creep out with their heavy secrets/ to the war 'that no one wants'."

The poem "American Dreams" brings up another matter of interest that makes it necessary to reproduce the poem in order to demonstrate why it, apart from being a war and American piece, deserves attention:

> In dreams my life came toward me,
> my loves that were slender as gazelles.
> But America also dreams. . . .
> Dream, you are flying over Russia,
> dream, you are falling in Asia.
>
> .   .   .
>
> As I look down the street
> on a typical sunny day in California
> it is my house that is burning
> and my dear ones that lie in the gutter
> as the American army enters.

> Every day I wake far away
> from my life, in a foreign country.
> These people are speaking a strange language.
> It is strange to me
> and strange, I think, even to themselves.

"American Dreams" was first published in the Spring, 1960, issue of *Listen* and Simpson could have included it, therefore, in
either *At the End of the Open Road* or *Selected Poems*; but he
chose not to do so. From the time America began its increased
military involvement in Southeast Asia, the poem has been frequently reprinted. For example, it appeared in an article titled
"Poetry of the Read-In Campaign" in the May 30, 1966, number
of *The Nation*; it was also reprinted in the September 16, 1966,
number of *Peace News*; and, since 1966, it has been reprinted
often in anthologies of current American and/or antiwar poetry.
The poem as a statement of protest to American military involvement in Vietnam obviously accounts for some of the frequency of
its being reproduced. But Simpson did not write the poem for this
reason. He wrote it, I should imagine, as another ironic indictment
of the American need to expand.

In "Doubting," Simpson contrasts the exuberant feelings he held
when he first came to America in 1940 with those he owns now;
and the main one now is perhaps best characterized as loss, as if
the promise America held for him and for others simply was not
fulfilled. The poem concludes with the speaker in a depressed
state, giving into the loss, having had to "learn to be patient with
the soul,/ breathe in, breathe out,/ and to sit by the bed and
watch." Coupled with the speaker's desires to kill himself, to kill
others, and to commit fanatical acts, and coupled with other instances in this volume that draw situations from his six-month
hospital stay after World War II and that draw from the institu-
tionalizing of others—these lines suggest that Simpson's delayed
combat fatigue after the war must be held responsible to some
degree for the attitudes expressed in "Doubting," one being an
indictment of "wars of democracy." George Washington and
Thomas Jefferson are invoked for their responses to America's
presence in Vietnam: "They would think they were Hessians,/ and
ride back into the hills/ to find the people that they knew."

One of the most interesting aspects of "Doubting" is Simpson's

having his speaker assume he is Walt Whitman commenting on
America as it now is, or if not Whitman, then a mock-Whitman:

> I myself am the union of these states,
> offering liberty and equality to all.
> I share the land equally, I support the arts,
>
> I am developing backward areas.
> I look on the negro as myself, I accuse myself
> of sociopathic tendencies, I accuse my accusers.
>
> I write encyclopedias and I revise the encyclopedias.
> Inside myself there is a record-breaking shot-putter and a
>   track team in training.
>
> I send up rockets to the stars.

After this Simpson-Whitman identification, the speaker concludes
the poem with the lines suggesting mental confinement. "Doubting" must stand surely as one of Simpson's most negative poems
about America.

"Sacred Objects," written to celebrate Whitman's birthday ob-
servance at the Huntington Library in 1969, is one of the most
significant poems in *Adventures of the Letter I*. The poem is
keyed to Whitman's phrase "to form individuals," which, Simpson
contends in this poem (for the phrase appears also in "Doubting"), is "The light that shines through the *Leaves*." The reader's
attention is immediately engaged by the poem's ironically casual
opening: "I am taking part in a great experiment—/ whether
writers can live peacefully in the suburbs/ and not be bored to
death." What follows in the poem reveals something of the crea-
tive-writing process, at least something of Simpson's method, for
it is not the first instance of such a revelation in *Adventures of the
Letter I*. Whitman is introduced as having said,

>   an American muse
> installed amid the kitchen ware.
> And we have wonderful household appliances . . .
> now tell me about the poets.

The following passage is taken from "Things," which is included
in the New Poems division of *Selected Poems*, and reappears in
"Sacred Objects" in the context quoted above:

"Things which to us in the pure state are mysterious,
Are your simplest articles of household use—
A chair, a dish, and meaner even than these,
The very latest inventions.
Machines are the animals of the Americans—
Tell me about machines."

The second part of "Sacred Objects" places emphasis on Whitman commenting on "an American muse . . . ," in allusions to "A swamp where the seabirds brood," "the psyche," "the soul," and finally in a reference to Long Island Sound. Though these allusions are more or less tangential, the presence of Whitman is felt throughout in the speaker's attempt to find the essence of what it is to be a person, a poet, and an American—considerations Simpson treats in other poems of this kind. With these aims in mind, then, the poem is addressed to *you*, whose identification poses a mystery: perhaps it is Lucina of line eight—"Where are your children, Lucina?"; perhaps it is Whitman; perhaps it is *you* in the sense of *you-me-everyman*. Whatever the case may be, the speaker declares, "And the kingdom is within you . . . / the hills and all the streams/ running west to the Mississippi," which is followed by a passage of considerable lyric strength:

There the roads are lined with timothy
and the clouds are tangled with the haystacks.

Your loves are a line of birch trees.
When the wind flattens the grass, it
shines, and a butterfly
writes dark lines on the air.

There are your sacred objects,
the wings and gazing eyes
of the life you really have.

"Sacred Objects" could have ended here with the inner life imaged in delicate perceptions of the natural world. However, Simpson is not satisfied with the ideal; instead, he forces us to concentrate on what, in fact, we are confronted with daily: drive-in restaurants, the smell of gasoline and asphalt, hot dogs, Pepsi Cola, the "monotonous grasshoppers" of our lives—all of which are included in Part III of the poem.

III   *Jamaica and the Turning Inward*

With the exception of "My Father in the Night Commanding No" from *At the End of the Open Road,* Simpson had not placed in his books any poems concerning his early years in Jamaica until the several poems in this volume, the best of which is "The Island Mentality." Divided into three sections, this poem relates three incidents, two of which Simpson has definitely written about before (see Chapter 1); and the possibility exists that he has also written about the third. The first concerns his father's having set up the telescope when Simpson was four or five years old; the effect was, as Simpson once wrote, that he become "moonstruck and devoted to poetry"; the second incident concerns the drowning of some forty natives when an excursion launch sank in the Kingston harbor; and the third episode concerns Simpson and a girl named Maud who together watched natives dancing. The girl may be his first love (see Chapter 1), whom he met when he was about twelve years old and whom he remembers as having been in and out of his dreams for years following.

The most notable characteristics of this lyric sequence are the fragmentary quality of the images and rhythms, the indictment of the superior attitude the colonists held toward the natives, and the colonists' lack of feeling toward the tragedy of the excursion launch. These characteristics can best be exemplified by the following excerpt from Part II:

> O I don't know
> says the Duke
> I think it's a lot of belly rot
>
> blue sand
> white waves
> jolly good chaps
> in nigger graves.

Since Simpson once intended calling this book *An American Peasant,* it is not surprising to find a poem bearing this title. Naturally, the American peasant is Simpson, who in the poem first meets with a friend, a revolutionary who argues "about Black Power/ Che Guevara, the SDS," but then the speaker prefers to observe phenomena on Fifth Avenue in New York, the setting of the poem, rather than to listen to the revolutionary. That the speaker is more concerned with outside events than with his friend's overwhelming pronouncements prompts the latter to exclaim, "What's the use . . . you're not listening!" Which is absolutely right and which acts as a catalyst for Simpson to state outrightly his "position," or lack of it. But even this statement is tempered by irony, as if Simpson is holding back from looking at himself too seriously:

> You're right. I have always lived
> as though I knew the reason.
> Like a peasant I trust in silence.
> And I don't believe in ideas
> unless they are unavoidable.

> Only yesterday, Thanksgiving,
> in the middle of dinner
> as I rocked to and fro with a toothache,
> my wife said, 'At last
> you have learned *dahvinen* . . . to pray.'

This turning inward toward himself is, as I mentioned in the introductory portion of this chapter, more characteristic of the poems in *Adventures of the Letter I* than of those in his earlier volumes. It is found in a number of the poems—several, for instance, in which Simpson considers for the first time directly the subject of mental illness.[2] "Permission to Operate a Motor Vehicle," "Simplicity," and "Cynthia" are poems that fit into this category and that are interesting primarily for this reason. Other than the subject of mental illness—his and others—two additional poems belong in the personal groupings: "Sensibility" and "Vandergast and the Girl." The former is a small poem about the speaker's marrying a "tender girl" who wept and wept; the situation parallels the circumstances of Duncan Bell and his first wife, Libby, in the novel *Riverside Drive*. The latter is the story of a married man who had an affair and whose wife then took the children and left him. When, toward the end of the poem, the speaker asks, "Was it worth it?," he replies, "You'd have to be Vandergast, looking through his eyes/ at the house across the street in Orange, New Jersey." "In any case," the speaker dryly concludes, "he will soon be forty."

Other than the story of Vandergast, which could be the story of any man who fractured, perhaps unwittingly, the routine of his daily life, the poem includes a section, a digressive analogy, in which the speaker introduces his own past, the suggestion being that he too went the way of Vandergast, the further suggestion being that the actual telling of Vandergast's story is the speaker's way of trying to come to terms with what seemingly must have been a similar situation. The speaker uses the word *definitions* to get at the issue: "Vandergast says he never intended/ having an affair," which draws this speaker response:

> And was that what this was?
> The names that people give to things. . . .
> What do definitions and divorce-court proceedings
> have to do with breathless reality?

For eleven lines the speaker then addresses a woman in his past with whom he had, or so we are led to believe, an affair. It should be noted that in 1954 Simpson and his first wife were divorced (Simpson was forty-one at the time) and that in his novel Mona and Duncan Bell carry on an affair while Duncan is married to Libby (the marriage ends in divorce). The novel is to an extent autobiographical, and it is possible that Simpson is both the speaker of this poem and Vandergast; that is, Vandergast *may be* considered a projection of sorts of Simpson. Clearly there are outstanding differences between the two. At any rate, although this kind of autobiographical criticism is of some interest, it is hardly germane to an understanding of the dual emotions of pathos and confusion underscoring the poem.

IV "A Friend of the Family"

In five sections and with 119 lines, "A Friend of the Family" is the longest poem of the volume and one of the most significant; for it brings together a number of Simpson's familiar subjects, themes, and attitudes. The poem begins with a Simpson trademark: an ironic attack on American materialism as it manifests itself in California. In this instance, the attack follows a seemingly cruel opening to the poem: "Once upon a time in California/ the ignorant married the inane/ and they lived happily ever after." Out of context and certainly as the beginning of a poem, these lines read like an intellectual snob's condescending appraisal of ill-equipped mentalities; but Simpson's speaker means exactly what he says. There is no irony involved, the proof of which resides in the contrast beginning with the word *But* in the next stanza and in this excerpt from "Walt Whitman at Bear Mountain," a poem in which America's plunge into materialistic progress is the object of the poet's indictment: "But the man who keeps a store on a lonely road,/ And the housewife who knows she's dumb,/ And the earth, are relieved" [from the charge of having contracted the disease of "American dreams"]. Here is the conflict as it appears in the second stanza of "A Friend of the Family":

> But nowadays in the villas
> with swimming-pools shaped like a kidney
> technicians are beating their wives.
> They're accusing each other of mental cruelty.

Then attention is called to the "children of those parents," children to whom the present is too much with which to contend: "They want to get back to the good old days," the speaker ironically remarks. The means by which they seek to escape from the cruelties enacted in the family situation are instanced in a girl named Cyd, who, after leaving a convent (itself a place for escape), sought refuge in California and now "drifts from pad to pad," asking strangers for money—money to buy a hamburger, "Really."

We learn in Part II that America's materialistic nature has gotten the country into trouble: "The dynamo howls/ but the psyche is still, like an Indian." Simpson is, of course, reiterating the thematic thrusts of his California-Whitman poems in *At the End of the Open Road*. Since "A Friend of the Family" was written after the American sortie into Southeast Asia (the California-Whitman poems before it), Simpson has even more evidence than before with which to accuse; and the indictment continues:

> And those who are still distending the empire
> have vanished beyond our sight.
> Far from the sense of hearing
> and touch, they are merging
> with Asia . . .
>
> expanding the war on nature
> and the know-how to Asia.

The weakest division of the poem, Part III, begins with the question, "What are they doing in Russia/ these nights for entertainment?" The question is posed for two reasons: (1) to suggest that Russians are also materialistically programmed; (2) to provide the speaker with the opportunity to continue his attack on contemporary America by citing gas pumps that shine in the desert where women dye their hair. The character Chichikov is introduced as the symbolic embodiment of the misadventures of Progress. (A character in Nikolai Gogol's *Dead Souls*, Chichikov is both crafty and ambitious. He sees a way to become a wealthy landowner through buying up "dead souls," serfs who have died since the last census and who are therefore not officially dead.) The point of Part III is that we have enough absurdities "right here on earth"; we simply do not need to bumble into outer space.

Part IV begins by playfully mimicking T. S. Eliot: "Andrei, that fish you caught was my uncle," after which the speaker relates the story of his uncle's visit to Chekhov's house on the day the playwright died. Returning without having seen Chekhov, his uncle led an ordinary life until World War II: "Then, when Hitler sent for the Jews/ he said, 'And don't forget Isidor . . . / turn left at the pickle-factory.' " This passage refers directly to the poem "Isidor" in the Volhynia Province division of *Adventures of the Letter I*. Andrei is the contemporary Russian poet Andrei Voznesensky, whom Simpson has met and who is the object of address a second time in Part IV: "Andrei, all my life I've been haunted/ by Russia—a plain,/ a cold wind from the *shtetl*," which reminds us of the following sentence from the prefatory prose note to the Volhynia Province division: "I have come to think of the country around Lutsk . . . as a muddy plain with a dismal climate." From this point on in the poem, Simpson as the speaker becomes, as nearly as he can, one with his family in Volhynia. This identification, repeatedly alluded to in other poems, particularly in "Dvonya," is given a moving voice in the lines closing this section of the poem:

> In the night where candles shine
> I have a luminous family . . .
> people with their arms round each other
>
> forever.

We are not surprised in Part V when the speaker transports himself back to the time of his uncle and himself visits Chekhov, who becomes the subject of the concluding division and who, indeed, is the *Friend* of the title. Chekhov's house becomes symbolic of the heterogeneity of life itself; in addition, it is Chekhov's mind filled "with ideas," with characters in whom vanities of the human condition are waiting to be found:

> These idiots rule the world,
> Chekhov knew it, and yet
> I think he was happy, on his street.
> People live here . . . you'd be amazed.

And so the poem ends. But, before we encounter this curious acceptance of life, there is a two-line stanza taken from "In the Time of Villa," the final poem in *Selected Poems*. The passages follow:

> "Tell us, what is it you do exactly
> To justify your existence?"
> ["In the Time of Villa"]

> And the people who say, 'Tell us,
> what is it you do exactly to justify your existence?'
> ["A Friend of the Family"]

In both contexts, the question is pointed toward a justification of the value of writing, and the implication is that a writer is suspect, for his product is only literature.

CHAPTER *8*

Riverside Drive

LOUIS SIMPSON has said that his only published novel, *River-side Drive* (1962), is thinly autobiographical; but there is a remarkable parallel between the life of Duncan Bell, the narrator-protagonist, and Simpson himself, which suggests that autobiography has indeed provided a firm basis for the novel. Before the narrative proper of *Riverside Drive* begins, the experiences of Duncan as a youth in Jamaica also are those of Simpson. Duncan's father and mother, who never appear as characters in the novel, are Simpson's parents. The preparatory school Duncan attended in the mountains of Jamaica was Simpson's Munro College. The incident of the motor-launch tragedy in Jamaica and the meager legacy the father bequeathed to his two sons—these and more belong to the lives of both Duncan and Simpson. Other than the personal tragedy of a family dissolved, the reasons Duncan cites for leaving Jamaica and coming to America are identical to those the poet has given, which have been discussed at some length in the first chapter of this study.

Duncan, as the narrative begins, is about the same age that Simpson was when he first arrived in New York City. At nineteen, Duncan is enrolled in a university in New York City, presumably Columbia, the school Simpson attended. In addition, both Duncan and Simpson serve in the 101st. Airborne Division in the glider infantry in World War II, suffer mental breakdowns after the war that result in hospital confinement, spend a year (1948) in Paris supposedly studying at the Sorbonne, return to New York, go to work for a publishing house, marry, are divorced, re-marry, and move to California where *Riverside Drive* ends and where Simpson was living when it was published.

There are differences, however, in the lives of Duncan Bell and Louis Simpson. Simpson returned to Columbia University where he took three degrees; Duncan never returns to college. The most

important difference, however, is that Duncan never writes poetry. He translates Racine and writes fiction, both of which are
credited as well to Simpson; but, unlike his life counterpart, Duncan achieves no measure of success from his writings. It would
seem merely an exercise in expressive criticism to document fully
the similarities and differences between the lives in question. It
suffices here to say that the parallels are close.

I *Mona*

Riverside Drive is not just the story of a young man between
the ages of nineteen and twenty-nine who is trying to come to
meaningful terms with himself; it is, in addition, the story of a
consuming love affair between Duncan Bell and Mona Jocelyn,
an enigmatic and desirable girl five years younger than Duncan.
She enters the narrative on the fourth page and does not leave
permanently until the end of the seventeenth chapter, which is
essentially the close of the narrative movement. The final chapter
is primarily an epilogue, an exposition of sorts, about what Duncan manages to do with his life after the inevitable breakup between Mona and him finally occurs. Mona does not appear in
every chapter, but she is nonetheless the compelling force in
Duncan's life.[1]

Duncan and Mona meet by chance on Riverside Drive in New
York City as she is walking her dog. The nineteen-year-old Duncan is unaware then that Mona is only fourteen years old (he
thinks she is more nearly his age); he only learns of her age when
he meets her after the war and after his subsequent confinement
in a mental institution. At the outset, Duncan is drawn physically
to Mona, an attraction that never diminishes. As the novel progresses, Mona becomes for him a composite of all women, but
primarily she is the embodiment of sexuality—even at the age of
fourteen.

Duncan first has doubts concerning Mona's promiscuity when
one of his friends at college, a boy named Gil, tells him that
Mona and a young man were once passionately embracing in a
bus he was on. When Duncan next sees Mona, he tells her that
he does not want to see her again; but he does not tell Mona why.
During the five-month period after the war while Duncan is
mentally cracking, he sees Mona regularly, but he has no memory

of this period in his life. Mona later explains that during this time Duncan wanted to marry her. Her parents, however, were opposed to the match; and his confinement put an end to the matter.

After his release from the hospital, Duncan secures a job with an import-export firm, finds an apartment for which his Uncle Herman generously pays the rent, calls Mona, and meets her in a restaurant. She tells of their rendezvous during the five-month blackout and asks why, several years ago, he broke off their friendship without a word of explanation. Duncan explains, and Mona abruptly dismisses Gil's story as being completely false.

Duncan's reaction to their first sexual union explains, in part, his attraction to Mona:

> Had I ever thought life monotonous? Had I ever felt that I would never be young? That was in another country, and the wench was very much alive. Holy God! Had I ever thought that imagination surpassed reality? She surpassed imagination, as greatest did least. Who could ever have imagined her? No pre-conception could match the beauty of my mistress as it had emerged from the garments that fell so lightly. The shape of a knee, the contour of a breast, were more than all the works of man. How did anything like business ever get done in the world? For my part, I could spend the rest of my time with Mona, letting the world go by. My room, and the city under the moon, and the moon herself, were illusions. How had this secret been kept? Why had no one ever described love? Oh, yes, a few had tried— Shakespeare had had something to say about it, but he hadn't had Mona.

After Mona is sent by her parents to a boarding school in Phila-delphia, Duncan continues to work at a job he is finding more and more intolerable. Unhappy in his work and disturbed that he can only see Mona infrequently, Duncan decides to study for a year at the Sorbonne; his education is paid for by the G.I. Bill, and his living expenses are assured by a government pension for his disability suffered during the war. He meets Libby Prames on the Rivera and comes to her aid when her girl friend and traveling companion absconds with Libby's money and jewelry. Returned to New York, Duncan, now determined to make something out of himself and his life, begins to keep regular company with Libby, whose father is extremely wealthy, and marries her.

Shortly after the marriage they separate, for the marriage has been wrong in every way. In fact, Duncan cannot tolerate Libby, who is both sexless and highly nervous. In any event, after they have been separated, Duncan again encounters Mona by chance; and ten years have passed since they first met.

The last quarter of *Riverside Drive* is devoted to Mona; the life Duncan leads is important to him only insofar as it relates to her. She is now in show business, a "part of the scenery" on a television variety show. Now, Duncan is nearly thirty; Mona is twenty-four. And once again, Mona's spell envelops Duncan. After the mismatch with Libby and the tour of rented rooms that followed, he is quite ready to accede to her presence. But Duncan slowly discovers contradictions in Mona. When she talks of show business, her voice sounds tinny, which repulses him. He begins to suspect that Mona "was not as far removed from the vulgarity of that life as she said she was." When they join physically, she seems "to be revenging herself on the world that, as she told me, though I found it hard to believe, disliked her." Duncan learns that for the past two years she has been seeing a psychiatrist. Then one night, Mona and Duncan engage in sexual intercourse on the living-room floor of the apartment she and her mother (her father is now dead) share while her mother is sleeping in her bedroom just down the corridor: "Apparently she had problems, as she had tried to tell me," Duncan dryly concludes.

Despite this growing knowledge that Mona's basic nature eludes him, Duncan still is with her as much as possible. Their relationship now is more than physical, but that element is still important. She becomes more than ever the symbolic embodiment of all women, physically, emotionally, and spiritually:

When I think of Mona, I see a number of women who, by some chance, have the features of one woman, as though the artist had only one idea of a nose, of eyes and ears, through which to show a variety of lives. As for cause and effect, chronology, it doesn't exist; or rather, it depends on the way I move the light. One of these women is chaste; another is unfaithful; a third is intelligent; a fourth is stupid. . . . When I think of Mona, pleasure and boredom, trust and suspicion, love and hatred, exist side by side, rapidly succeeding or merging into one another. Sometimes the light moves back again to fasten on a detail. And then, areas of the painting have faded.

Her promiscuity has been a search for herself—or rather, an attempt to get rid of the separate, contradictory selves that embroiled her in lies and quarrels, by attaching them to one man after another.

It is not surprising, then, that the relationship eventually dissolves; however, it is Mona, not Duncan, who initiates the break-up. She has become the "property" of one of the directors for whom she works, and she is anxious to let Duncan go. Duncan, of course, recovers after she tells him, "I don't want to see you again." After the affair is over, he appraises the story he has told: "Now I know that what I have told is the commonest story. Every other poor clerk, every other stenographer, knows as much. There is nothing new under the sun or under the moon, and the passion we feel is unique, the pain we feel time will never erase, for it is ours alone, has been felt by countless others. If we only knew how to speak to each other, we would find that we understand each other, for we have all loved a particular thing with all our heart and lost it. It is from this point that we begin our real lives."

II *War*

Duncan Bell is unable to remember much about his war experiences because of amnesia suffered during his period of mental disability after the war. What Duncan does remember, however, provides a valuable chronicle of a soldier's response to an entity over which he has no control and of which he really does not understand any more than what the perimeter of his vision and the range of his hearing allow. Duncan seems to be the average soldier, the one for whom war and the steps by which the military prepares one for it seem ridiculous. The correlation between the combat incidents recorded in *Riverside Drive*, in Louis Simpson's war poems, and in the essays about his experiences in the military during World War II is nearly exact. In fact, the parallel between Duncan and Simpson is so close in matters of war that it would seem merely an academic exercise to document the comparison. It is more interesting and profitable for the sake of literature to examine the military and war as Duncan knew them and to explore the important similarities between Duncan's exposure in *Riverside Drive* and Simpson's war poems, especially "The Runner."

In his factual, prose accounts of military life, Simpson stresses the senselessness of the details for which the soldier is held accountable by his superiors. This soldier is nothing but a follower of orders, and they often seem absurd ones. The attitude that the soldier is a pawn-child who is at the mercy of absolute authority and who has nothing to say about his fate prevails in Simpson's war lyrics written early in his career. In *Riverside Drive*, Duncan frequently voices his complaints about the details and the insults to which the soldier is subject.

The ambush depicted in "Carentan O Carentan" included in *The Arrivistes* occurs also in *Riverside Drive;* the similarities between the ways in which the situation is described are interesting. Here are lines five through ten of the poem:

> This was the shining green canal
> Where we came two by two
> Walking at combat-interval.
> Such trees we never knew.
>
> The day was early June, the ground
> Was soft and bright with dew.

The following passage from *Riverside Drive* describes the soldiers after just having embarked from the gliders: "And now in two files, at combat interval, we are walking up the slope. . . . There are green fields sparkling in the cool, dewy air of June; there are hedgerows and apple trees." Two pages further in the novel, the ambush takes place, and the men are initiated into the possibility of their own deaths. The happenings in the poem "Carentan O Carentan" provide the substance for a dream Duncan had in Paris several years after the conclusion of the war.

The narrator of "The Runner" seems to be Louis Simpson, but the experiences of the protagonist Dodd parallel, in large measure, what Simpson himself experienced as an infantry soldier in the 101st. Airborne Division during the defense of Bastogne in December, 1944. Duncan Bell, then, seems to assume the persons of both the narrator and protagonist of "The Runner"; there is, however, one significant difference. In a moment of panic, Dodd, unlike both Simpson and Duncan, appears to act as a coward, and this act provides the essential conflict in the poem. Otherwise, the characters and the experiences of Dodd and Duncan are parallel, as numerous parallel passages indicate. Two brief passages serve to illustrate this correspondence between novel and poem better than any man's explanatory prose.

(1) *Riverside Drive*

As we approached a house set off by itself in an orchard, we came upon a plump mattress dragged out under a tree with a German officer stretched on it. He had been laid there to die in all possible comfort. The mattress feathers were escaping through a tear in the material, littering the grass. . . . he had swollen, and was continuing to swell. His belt was lost in the balloon of his belly. His legs and arms stuck straight out; his fingers were plump as carrots. His legs were stuffed into the boots that would, it appeared, split at any moment.

"The Runner"

> Houses stood here and there.
> In front of one, a mattress had been laid,
> And on the mattress, a German officer.
> He was puffed up with air like a balloon,
> Belly and limbs swelling as if to split
> His uniform. The grass was stuck with feathers.

(2) *Riverside Drive*

A little further on in a field a Messerschmidt had crashed on its nose. Delicately it hung there, the black crosses glaring from the fuselage.

"The Runner"

> Beyond the wood there stretched an open road.
> They filed out on it. In a field of hay
> A place perched on its nose, a *Messerschmidt*,
> The black cross glaring.

I offer the final passage from the war narrative of *Riverside Drive* as a summary statement for Louis Simpson about war; it serves, as well, for his poems and essays on the subject and marks him as a major literary interpreter of war:

Someday, I thought, after the professionals have finished with it, I'm going to tell the story of the real war. There won't be anything but cold, rain, and men falling into tent walls in the dark.

Why not go further? Tell it from the viewpoint of the materials—the shovel, the mud, the hole in the mud.

Of course, I have not told this story. It would be unendurably monotonous, as war itself is monotonous. But physical discomfort may be the ultimate horror. All that we have so elaborately constructed over the centuries—the roof above our heads, and the roof of ideas—is removed, and there we stand, like so many forked radishes, exposed to rain and wind and snow. It is not only the poor naked wretches under the eye of the Germans, men, women, and children, as they stumble, hand in hand, toward the gas chambers, who have been degraded. All of us have lost our covering. And with it, the mystery that alone keeps men sane.

III   *The Continent and Some Poems*

Since we can assume that Louis Simpson was writing *Riverside Drive* over a period of years prior to its 1962 publication, it is not surprising that the novel is not charged with the subject of America, as his poems from 1959 are. Nevertheless, there are some specific situations, expressions, and images in *Riverside Drive* that occur in some of the America poems. Early in the narrative, Duncan tells of his wish, on first coming to America, to immerse himself into the spirit of the country: "When I came to America, the democracy of labor changed my ideas. My mind went out to meet democracy and leaped beyond. America, I thought, meant revolution—a new world. I was committed to America. I had a convert's belief that everything in this new life was different and better; even the way people blew their noses was interesting. At every turn there were gestures I did not understand. I wanted to understand the unifying principle of this life; surely there was a secret which, if I knew it, would explain everything."

In the third stanza of the poem "There Is," which first appeared in a 1960 number of *Listen* under the title "Look! From My Window," and which is included in *At the End of the Open Road* under the revised title, we find this passage which parallels the one just quoted from the novel:

> But I have no profession. Like a spy
> I read the papers—Situations Wanted.
> Surely there is a secret
> which, if I knew it, would change everything!

The expression "I have no profession" also occurs elsewhere in the novel. Further on in the narrative, Duncan tells of walks in the summer twilight that he and Mona took along *Riverside Drive:* "The couples we passed seemed enervated with the same drowsy passion. There was a conspiracy in the dusk, in all the corners of the park. From the darkness beyond the halos of lamplight, the laugh of a woman and the insistent pleading of a man were borne lazily to our ears. The air was filled with Eros, whispering." And, in the seventh stanza of "There Is," we read:

> When darkness falls on the enormous street
> the air is filled with Eros, whispering.
> Eyes, mouths, contrive to meet
> in silence, fearing they may be prevented.

I have no idea which came first to Simpson—the poem or the novel passages.

There are additional parallels between the poems and the novels, excluding the poems in which a Mona-like woman figures and excluding the analogous war poems. One of the more interesting and the last parallel I choose to cite occurs in the last page of *Riverside Drive* and in the closing statement of "Stumpfoot on 42nd Street," which was first printed in *Choice* in 1965 and which is included in the New Poems section of *Selected Poems.* Duncan Bell concludes his story with this brief paragraph: "Just by being alive we change the world. We aren't responsible for everything. And perhaps it is enough simply to exist." On these terms Duncan finally comes to accept himself—the same terms, it appears, that the speaker of the poem discerns apply to Stumpfoot: "It seems that a man exists/ Only to say, Here I am in person."

IV *Meaning and Value*

We come to know Duncan Bell as a kind of anti-hero. In no way is he presented as having qualities developed to the extent of public distinction. In fact, he is a "loser"; but he is an intelligent, sensitive, and introspective "loser." He possesses those qualities by which it is difficult to achieve any sort of recognition, which, of course, Duncan does not seek. He wants Mona, whom he is forced to relinquish, and he wants simply to live with some degree of personal satisfaction.

There are several significant turning points in the life of Duncan, apart from the ones in which Mona is inexorably involved, the first one taking place in a hotel room in Paris in 1948 where Duncan has been waiting for a woman with whom he arranged an assignation earlier in the evening. She never appears; and, at three o'clock in the morning, he begins to see how ridiculous both he and his situation surely must seem: "There must be something wrong with my character," he says. Then his past flashes before him as if on a screen, after which he comes to this realization: "Then, like a gust of fresh air, I admitted the truth: I had been ridiculous, and there was nothing I could do about it now." Once expurgated of his own anxieties, Duncan's mind then flashes with scenes of life, images from the world of people alive in the fullest sense, and he comes to terms with acceptance: "I have been taking myself too seriously, I thought. From now on, I'm going to expect less of myself, forgive my mistakes, accept my own humanity." He then resolves to remove himself "from the influence of aimless or deluded characters," as he had rid himself shortly before of his illusions. At the age of forty, he ruminates, he might "be a decent, productive member of society." Unfortunately, his good intentions bring him into a marriage with Libby Prames.

The marriage is simply a failure, though Libby tries in her bungling way to make it work. The missing element is love on the part of Duncan, whose private life with Libby is a raw nerve. The only solace he finds is in his work with the Hancock-Williams Press, but it is not enough for Duncan, who has known love before, to resign himself to a five-day life. He reaches the point, however, where he welcomes Monday mornings and dreads Friday evenings. Thus the next major turning point in his life is the decision to leave Libby and to make some kind of life for himself: "Now I must begin all over again. I must assume the responsibility for my life. I must admit that I am visible and that what I do matters. I must make it matter."

Years after the Mona affair dissolved, Alec Litvin, Duncan's leftist friend whom he had not seen for nearly ten years, pays a visit to Valencia, California, where Duncan and his second wife are living. Duncan tries to explain why he is now working for the Institute for Handicapped Children and fills Alec in on the external details of his life. He is unable, however, to tell him of the decisions that mattered:

I explained these things, but I couldn't tell him why I'd changed my life. There came a time when I realized that everything I'd always thought I wanted was no longer necessary. An unhappy love affair was part of the story; but there were other influences. In New York I would never have been better than second-rate. I didn't have the drive it takes; or perhaps I was too honest to manipulate words and symbols in order to get power—the occupation of men like myself, professional men without a profession. And the dream of being a writer—like the dream of piano or violin playing that used to be inculcated in children by their mothers and served only to embitter their lives—this too I had abandoned. For I lacked the originality and sheer stamina it takes. So one night in New York I dropped my manuscripts down the incinerator chute, and as I heard them thumping into the fire, I felt that a load had been lifted off my shoulders.

But maybe it was love, after all. I was tired of love, tired of trying to find happiness there. I was exhausted by feelings. In our time we put too much stress on love; we expect it to bear the weight of the sky, to do the work that used to be shared out among princes and servants, angels, demons, poets, hangmen, philosophers, and slaves. Feelings are all we have left, and love is the field to which we march. We are dying of human relationships.

An ironically significant justice is at work in Duncan's explanation. Some years before, when he confided to Libby's father that the marriage was a failure, Mr. Prames told Duncan that the younger man could have anything in life that he wanted if he were willing to give up that which he wanted most. Mr. Prames said that he had done this when, as a young man, he came to the realization that he had neither the drive nor the ability to become a first-rate artist, and subsequently gave up art. It seems that this is what Duncan finally decides to do, though he has to drop Libby on the way toward doing so.

Riverside Drive thus chronicles Duncan Bell's publicly insignificant but nevertheless privately fascinating life: insignificant in that his presence makes little difference to the world; fascinating in that he experiences war, confinement in a mental institution, and a consuming love affair. If the novel tells us anything about ourselves and the daily business of living, its message must be that every human being deserves attention, if only because he *is* a human being. There are collateral lessons, too: war is inane, wrecking its initiates both physically and mentally; and, if it does not actually wreck them, it scars them as perhaps no other form of human behavior can. Love is the most exciting experience in life; but, at the same time, it can be both debilitating and obsessive when it becomes the controlling factor in one's life.

In a May 9, 1962, review of *Riverside Drive* for the New York *Herald Tribune,* John K. Kutchens cites several qualities distinguishing the novel that are found also in Louis Simpson's poetry: "a firm intelligence, a spare, intense way with words, a gift for images used with a difference." The prose is indeed replete with instances of "images used with a difference," a characteristic to which the following passage ably testifies: "Exiting from the popcorn *palazzi,* avidly I inhaled the cold air of the winter streets and made for the nearest subway station, passing cigar stores and drugstores weeping in neon, like the lines of a face gone wrong, running with tears of electricity, blinking sadly through the dusk. I lost count, in those dim interiors [in movie theaters where he worked as a "spy" for the management], of the divisions of day and night. . . ."

The first three volumes of Simpson's poetry abound in poems shining with ironic humor. The irony remains in the fourth volume, *At the End of the Open Road,* and in the poems following to date; but the humor, largely a matter of dry, understated wit, is not as apparent. Like the early poetry, *Riverside Drive* can be humorous, most of its humor deriving from situations involving the marriage of Duncan and Libby, as in this instance: "Libby likes eating in Longchamps, the rich man's Childs. We lunch in a crowd of women, all eating what looks like lettuce covered with marshmallow whip. Someday I intend to vomit in Longchamps. But not today. Any place where they charge you extra for a slice of bread. . . ."

Riverside Drive is a good novel. To serious students of Louis Simpson, it is an important novel for the reasons that prompted the discussion of parallels in this chapter. The novel contains, I am convinced, much autobiographical material—despite Simpson's charge that *Riverside Drive* is only thinly autobiographical. The novel confirms, among other things, the thematic judgments his poems on war make; and its style is superior. The reviewer for the June, 1962, issue of *Harper's Magazine* makes these interesting observations: "*Riverside Drive* is a graceful, delicate, tender

book, unpretentious and free of theatricality. The worst to be
said about it is also perhaps the best; it is more the work of a
poet than of a novelist." This last statement is a form of un-
equivocal praise.

CHAPTER *9*

Conclusion: The Life Within

R IVERSIDE DRIVE can be read in part as a fictionalized account of some of the events in Louis Simpson's life considered in the first chapter of this study, events that surely have helped to shape the poems for which he will be chiefly remembered in any literary history of the period. No doubt his poem "Walt Whitman at Bear Mountain" will always accompany Simpson in any future appraisal of his contributions to American literature. And there will be other poems too—poems that are considerably better than good, such as "Carentan O Carentan" and "My Father in the Night Commanding No."

If it is true that a writer who understands and records the age in which he lives will be listened to by subsequent generations, then Simpson will always be heard. But he does more than chronicle his generation. His best war poems, for example, isolate and explore the forces working on the infantry soldier of World War II; they also universalize what war has always meant to men, but especially what war means to modern man, who must contend with the tools of war created by modern technology. The California-Whitman poems define the special qualities of the American character, spirit, and ethos; they also successfully juxtapose the past and the present, thereby revealing the disparities between what American traditionally has thought it was and what it is.

Simpson's poems divide sharply into two stylistic catagories: on the one hand, those demonstrating an expertise within the conventions; on the other, those exemplifying an abrupt departure from the conventions in which he worked so convincingly. It is within the latter category that much of Simpson's permanent contributions to American literature resides. He will continue to write poems in the natural voice of man, he will continue to rely on the efficacy of the image, and he will continue to go beneath the surface of his subjects to find the life within.

Notes and References

Chapter One

1. Anonymous, "Four Who Swim Through the Desert," *Columbia College Today* (Winter, 1964), 63.

2. "An Interview with Louis Simpson, Part II," *dust*, I (Winter, 1965), 21.

3. Unless otherwise noted, the material in this chapter concerning Simpson's family and his life in Jamaica is taken from information supplied by Simpson and from the following two articles: Duncan Bell [Louis Simpson], "The Wedding of Scotland and Poland," *Hudson Review*, XIII (Winter, 1960–61), 489–504. "Confessions of an American Poet," *New York Times Magazine*, May 2, 1965, pp. 30–31, 108–10.

4. "The Poet on his Work—2: 'How I wrote Returning,'" *Christian Science Monitor*, February 24, 1967.

5. "An Interview with Louis Simpson, Part II," pp. 15–16.

6. *Ibid.*, pp. 16–17.

7. "Four Who Swim Through the Desert," p. 63.

8. The discussion of Simpson's prewar military training is taken from the following article: "The Making of a Soldier USA," *Harper's Magazine*, CCXXXII (February, 1966), 76–80.

9. "The Way It Was In the Bulge," *New York Times Magazine*, December 6, 1964, pp. 27–29, 114, 116, 119, 122–24.

10. The discussion of Simpson's hospitalization is taken from "An Interview with Louis Simpson, Part II," pp. 21–23.

11. *Ibid.*, p. 22.

12. "Baudelaire in Three Injections," *Harper's Magazine*, CCXXX (June, 1965), 48–50.

13. "What's In It for Me (2)," *Harper's Magazine*, CCXXXI (October, 1965), 172.

14. "An Interview with Louis Simpson, Part II," pp. 10–14.

15. *Ibid.*, p. 11.

16. "An Interview with Louis Simpson, Part I," *dust*, I (Fall, 1964), 6.

17. "Confessions of an American Poet," p. 109.
18. "An Interview with Louis Simpson, Part I," p. 11.
19. "Four Who Swim Through the Desert," p. 63.
20. "An Interview with Louis Simpson, Part I," p. 11.
21. "What's In It for Me (2)," p. 172.

Chapter Two

1. Yohma Gray, "The Poetry of Louis Simpson," *Tri-Quarterly* V (Spring, 1963), 35.
2. *Ibid.*, p. 35.
3. Crunk [Robert Bly], "The Work of Louis Simpson," *Fifties,* 1st issue (1958), 24.
4. C. B. Cox, "The Poetry of Louis Simpson," *Critical Quarterly* VIII (Spring, 1966), 73.
5. "An Interview with Louis Simpson, Part II," p. 23.
6. Gray, p. 38.
7. "An Interview with Louis Simpson, Part II," p. 19.

Chapter Three

1. Donald Hall, "The New Poetry: Notes on the Past Fifteen Years in America," *New World Writing,* VII (April, 1955), 245.
2. Bly, "The Work of Louis Simpson," p. 25.
3. Thom Gunn, "American Examples," *Spectator* (March 27, 1957), p. 442.
4. Stephen Dunning, "Why Poetry?," *English Journal,* LV (February, 1966), 160.
5. *Ibid.*, p. 160.
6. Cox, p. 77.
7. Bly, "The Work of Louis Simpson," p. 25.
8. Cox, p. 77.
9. *Ibid.*, p. 78.
10. *Ibid.*, p. 77.

Chapter Four

1. Anthony Hecht, "The Anguish of the Spirit and the Letter," *Hudson Review,* XII (Winter, 1959–60), 597.
2. Donald Hall, "U. S. Poetry in England," *Encounter,* XV (September, 1960), 83.
3. Hecht, p. 598.
4. Bly, "The Work of Louis Simpson," p. 25.
5. Crunk [Robert Bly], "Louis Simpson's New Book," *Sixties,* IV (Fall, 1960), 59.
6. Norman Friedman, "The Wesleyan Poets—II," *Chicago Review,* XIX (1966), 68–69.

7. *Ibid.*, p. 69.

8. Even though "A Dream of Governors," the title poem of this collection, is not exemplary of Friedman's criticism as "The Green Shepherd" seems to be, the former is more an exercise in technique than a felt poem. I am therefore omitting it from my discussion.

9. Cox, p. 77.

10. Friedman, p. 67.

11. Hecht, p. 598.

12. Cox, p. 72.

13. Thom Gunn, "Excellence and Variety," *Yale Review,* XLIX (Winter 1960), pp. 298–99; Bly, "Louis Simpson's New Book," pp. 58–59; Cox, p. 72.

14. Philip Booth, *New York Times Book Review,* September 27, 1959, p. 22.

15. Bly, "Louis Simpson's New Book," p. 58.

16. Gray, pp. 36–37.

17. "An Interview with Louis Simpson, Part II," p. 19.

Chapter Five

1. Donald Hall, "Introduction," *Contemporary American Poetry* (Baltimore, 1962), p. 24.

2. The discussion that follows is taken from the following article: Ronald Moran and George Lensing, "The Emotive Imagination: A New Departure in American Poetry," *Southern Review,* III, n.s. (Winter, 1967), 51–67.

3. Gray, p. 35.

4. Duane Locke, "New Directions in Poetry," *dust,* 1 (Fall, 1964), 68–69.

5. *Ibid.*, p. 69.

6. Gray, p. 36.

7. R. R. Cuscaden, "In the Shark's Belly," *Today,* XXI (January, 1966), 14.

8. Friedman, p. 71.

9. Ronald Moran, "Time of Heterogeneity: A Chronicle of Fifteen," *Southern Review,* I, n.s. (Spring, 1965), 475–76.

10. Thom Gunn, "Modes of Control," *Yale Review,* LIII (Spring, 1964), 458.

11. William Stafford, "Terminations, Revelations," *Poetry,* CIV (May, 1964), 104.

12. Simpson told me that "On the Lawn at the Villa" came out of a meeting he had with his mother, who had remarried and was living in northern Italy. It was the first time he had seen her in nearly twenty years.

13. Gray, p. 36.
14. Cox, pp. 78–83.
15. Berchtesgaden is the resort village where Hitler's private retreat was located. Hitler does not figure in the poem.

Chapter Six

1. This poem is included as number 2 of the three-part sequence "Indian Country" in *Adventures of the Letter I*.

Chapter Seven

1. *Poet's Choice*, ed. Paul Engle and Joseph Langland (New York, 1962), p. 219.
2. "The Flight to Cytherea" from *A Dream of Governors* is a veiled account of his mental breakdown and is discussed at length in Chapter 4.

Chapter Eight

1. There are two allusions in *Riverside Drive* to Marcel Proust's *Swann's Way*, suggesting to some reviewers of the novel that the affair between Duncan and Mona owes a literary debt to Swann and Odette. To an extent, this indebtedness may be valid, but it does not seem of major importance to this study.

Selected Bibliography

PRIMARY SOURCES

1. Books

The Arrivistes: Poems 1940–1949. Privately printed in Paris but distributed by the Fine Editions Press in New York, 1949.
Good News of Death and Other Poems (in Poets of Today II). New York: Charles Scribner's Sons, 1955.
A Dream of Governors. Middletown: Wesleyan University Press, 1959.
James Hogg, A Critical Study. Edinburgh: Oliver & Boyd, 1962.
Riverside Drive. New York: Atheneum, 1962.
At the End of the Open Road. Middletown: Wesleyan University Press, 1963.
Selected Poems. New York: Harcourt, Brace & World, 1965.
An Introduction to Poetry. New York: St. Martin's Press, 1967.
Adventures of the Letter I. London: Oxford University Press, 1971.

2. Book Edited

The New Poets of England and America. Eds. Donald Hall, Robert Pack, [and] Louis Simpson. New York: Meridian Books, 1957.

3. Articles and Interviews

"Poets in Isolation," *Hudson Review,* X (Autumn, 1957), 458–64.
"In the Absence of Yeats," *Hudson Review,* XII (Summer, 1959), 308–14.
"A Garland for the Muse," *Hudson Review,* XIII (Summer, 1960), 284–93.
Under pseudonym of Duncan Bell, "The Wedding of Scotland and Poland," *Hudson Review,* XIII (Winter, 1960–61), 489–504.
"Important and Unimportant Poems," *Hudson Review,* XIV (Autumn, 1961), 461–70.
"Matters of Tact," *Hudson Review,* XIV (Winter, 1961–62), 614–17.
"Poetry Chronicle," *Hudson Review,* XVI (Spring, 1963), 130–40.

"An Interview with Louis Simpson, Part I," *dust*, I (Fall, 1964), 3–23.

"The Way It Was in the Bulge," *New York Times Magazine*, December 6, 1964, pp. 27–29, 114, 116, 119, 122–24.

"An Interview with Louis Simpson, Part II," *dust*, I (Winter, 1965), 9–24.

"Confessions of an American Poet," *New York Times Magazine*, May 2, 1965, pp. 30–31, 108–10.

"Baudelaire in Three Injections," *Harper's Magazine*, CCXXX (June 1965), 48–50.

"What's In It for Me (2)," *Harper's Magazine*, CCXXXI (October 1965), 172.

"The Making of a Soldier USA," *Harper's Magazine*, CCXXXII (February 1966), 76–80.

SECONDARY SOURCES

CRUNK [ROBERT BLY]. "The Work of Louis Simpson" *Fifties*, 1st Issue (1958), 22–25. Discussion of the early poems. Notes Simpson's reliance on following the traditions.

————. "Louis Simpson's New Book," *Sixties*, IV (Fall, 1960), 58–61. Review of *A Dream of Governors*. Finds inward excitement in the poems not in line with traditional forms employed. He wants Simpson to break from the traditions.

COX, C. B. "The Poetry of Louis Simpson," *Critical Quarterly*, VIII (Spring, 1966), 72–83. Analysis of characteristics distinguishing the poems. Thoroughly worked out explication of "Moving the Walls."

FRIEDMAN, NORMAN. "The Wesleyan Poets–II," *Chicago Review*, XIX (1966), 55–72. Analysis of books of poetry by James Dickey and Simpson (*A Dream of Governors* and *At the End of the Open Road*) published by Wesleyan University Press. Simpson rated as better poet than Dickey. Observes Simpson's change in style from first to second volume issued by Wesleyan; finds the new style an improvement.

GRAY, YOHMA. "The Poetry of Louis Simpson," *Tri-Quarterly*, V (Spring, 1963), 33–39. Discussion of poems up to those included in *At the End of the Open Road*, though the author considers several poems in magazines that were to be included in that volume.

LOCKE, DUANE. "New Directions in Poetry: The Work of Louis Simpson," *dust*, I (Fall, 1964), 67–69. Perceptive analysis of Simpson's altered style evident in *At the End of the Open Road*. Calls the new style "phenomenalism."

MORAN, RONALD. "Louis Simpson: The Absence of Criticism and The Presence of Poetry," *The Far Point*, I (Fall/Winter, 1968), 60–66.

Analysis of Simpson as a critic and his beliefs on the function and purpose of poetry. Cites observations Simpson makes on the current state of American poetry. (Author's note: Even though Simpson's criticism is valuable, it lies outside the definitive boundary of this book, which is a study of Simpson as a creative writer; therefore, I have not included his criticism for discussion.)

——. " 'Walt Whitman at Bear Mountain' and the American Illusion," *Concerning Poetry*, II (Spring, 1969), 5–9. An analysis of the poem taken from the discussion of it in Chapter 5 of this book.

MORAN, RONALD, and GEORGE LENSING. "The Emotive Imagination: A New Departure in American Poetry," *Southern Review*, III (Winter, 1967), 51–67. Analysis of poetry of Simpson, William Stafford, James Wright, and Robert Bly as representative of significant new movement in American poetry.

Index

(The works of Louis Simpson are listed under his name)